DAVID BERGER

Creative Jazz
Composing & Arranging III

WRITING *for* SMALL GROUPS

Such Sweet Thunder
Such Sweet Thunder Publishing
www.SuchSweetThunderMusic.com

Note to the Reader

Each chapter in this book includes full and partial recordings, an in-depth anlysis, and full scores. While I would have loved to provide everything in one place, the high cost of publishing such a package would have made it impossible for me to produce, and very expensive for you to buy.

In order to make this book affordable and practical, we have put the music videos and complete scores online. Each video shows pages from the score that you can follow as you read and listen. With the scores and videos separate from the text, you can easily go back and forth between them without having to turn pages.

Each score has a concert reduction added at the bottom of each page—all reeds and all brass parts are shown together, in concert key. Each reduction has tags showing the different techniques used.

♪ To download these recordings and scores free of charge, go to:
www.suchsweetthundermusic.com/pages/cjca3-accompanying-files

All the arrangements in this book are available at SuchSweetThunderMusic.com and all major digital music services.

PERSONNEL ON THE RECORDINGS

Conductor & Arranger:
　　David Berger
Reed 1 (Alto Sax, Clarinet, Flute)
　　Matt Hong
Reed 2 (Tenor Sax, Piccolo, Clarinet)
　　Dan Block
Reed 3 (Baritone Sax, Bass Clarinet)
　　Carl Maraghi
Trumpet　　Brian Pareschi
Trombone　Wayne Goodman
Piano　　　Isaac ben Ayala
Bass　　　 Sean Conley
Drums　　 Jimmy Madison
Vocal　　　Camille Thurman
Engineering　Fernando Lodeiro
Mixing　　 Oscar Zambrano
Mastering　Peter Axelsson

Recorded at The Hit Factory, New York City, October 22, 2021.

Creative Jazz Composing & Arranging III:
Writing For Small Groups
Copyright ©2023 by Such Sweet Thunder Publishing

All rights reserved. Printed in the United States of America. No part of this book may be used or reproduced in any manner whatsoever by any means, electronic or mechanical, including photocopying, recording, or by an information storage and retrieval system, without the written consent of the Publisher, except where permitted by law.

All the information in this book is published in good faith and for general information purposes only. David Berger and Such Sweet Thunder Publishing do not make any warranties about the completeness, reliability and accuracy of this information.

Any action you take based on the information you find herein is strictly at your own risk. David Berger and Such Sweet Thunder Publishing will not be liable for any losses and/or damages in connection with the use of this book.

If you require any more information or have any questions about this disclaimer, please feel free to contact us by email at:
information@SuchSweetThunderMusic.com

Book and Cover Design by
Nina Schwartz/Impulse Graphics
ISBN: 978-1-7335931-4-4
First Edition: November 30, 2023

Contents

Introduction iv

1. Definitions: Composing, Arranging, Orchestrating, Transcribing, Extracting 1
2. Basic Harmonization, Modulation and Creating a Lead Sheet 3
3. Four-Part Harmony 19
4. Mary's A Grand Old Name Quartet Arrangement (1 Horn) 27
5. Mary's A Grand Old Name Quintet Arrangement (2 Horns) . . . 45
6. Mary, Getting Grander Sextet Arrangement (3 Horns) 65
7. Mary, Even Grander Than That Octet Arrangement (5 Horns) 82
8. The Silver Bullet Octet Arrangement 99
9. Silver's Standard Octet Arrangement 127
10. In A Persian Market Octet Arrangement 147
11. Careless Love Octet Arrangement 179

Coda 210
Acknowledgements 212
Glossary 213
Index 223
About the Author 227
Other Books and CDs by David Berger 228
Book Reviews 229

Scores (Portrait Scores with Concert Reduction)
www.suchsweetthundermusic.com/pages/cjca3-accompanying-files

1. Mary's A Grand Old Name (Quartet)
2. Mary's A Grand Old Name (Quintet)
3. Mary's A Grand Old Name (Sextet)
4. Mary's A Grand Old Name (Octet)
5. The Silver Bullet (Octet)
6. Silver's Standard (Octet)
7. In A Persian Market (Octet)
8. Careless Love (Octet)

Videos
www.suchsweetthundermusic.com/pages/cjca3-accompanying-files

1. Mary's A Grand Old Name (Quartet)
2. Mary's A Grand Old Name (Quintet)
3. Mary's A Grand Old Name (Sextet)
4. Mary's A Grand Old Name (Octet)
5. The Silver Bullet (Octet)
6. Silver's Standard (Octet)
7. In A Persian Market (Octet)
8. Careless Love (Octet)

Introduction

In the fourth grade I took up the trumpet in school. Later that year I attended a concert at our elementary school. I'm sure the school chorus sang, but all I remember is our school band playing. I was mesmerized. I couldn't wait until the next year, when I could join the band.

During the concert, I had this amazing thought, "Wouldn't it be cool if I composed a piece for the band to play?" I can still see my 10-year-old self sitting in our auditorium that doubled as the gym. Don't ask me where that idea came from, but to this day it sticks with me. Wouldn't it be cool to write music and have musicians play it? After writing over 2000 arrangements and compositions, it's still cool. It's better than cool... it's why I wake up in the morning.

The act of writing music involves two processes. One is the logical physical expression of putting dots on pieces of paper that musicians will understand and interpret properly. The other is the mysterious creative process that imagines music that I would like to hear—what all the instruments (and singers) will sound like. Where the sounds in my head come from most likely is the tens of thousands of hours of listening and playing music. My memory has stored up these sounds, and then I let my subconscious mind mix them all up and spew out who-knows-what. In the process of getting these ideas onto paper in notation, I consciously impose the slightest bit of organization, so that it all makes sense. It is orderly, and yet surprising.

In my twenties, I studied trumpet with one of the greatest trumpet players of the 20th century, Jimmy Maxwell. When a student would call him on the phone and ask him if he taught how to play jazz, Jim's answer was, "I can teach you to improvise, but no one can teach you how to play jazz." Jazz is a special music that is inside us. It's personal.

In this book I will show you how to organize your thoughts and your music, but the music you will create depends on the music that has influenced you, and your willingness to unhook from your ego and tell the world your absolute truth. Hopefully, you will find this book encouraging in those regards.

My listening and study of music from Palestrina and Bach through Stravinsky and Bartók, and Jelly Roll Morton and Duke Ellington through Gil Evans has inspired me and set the high standards I aspire to. To paraphrase Sir Isaac Newton—
I've been standing on the shoulders of giants.

Learning to write music is a long process. It takes a lot of patience. When I was young, I read that that you learn more from your failures than your successes. Those failures hurt, but you never forget them. They push you to find workable solutions. Learning to arrange and compose jazz requires that you speak the language of jazz fluently—like a native.

When I grew up in the 1950's, I didn't hear much jazz, but I heard lots of classical music and swing music. The classical music was on a superior aesthetic level, but somehow, it didn't speak to me as an American. Swing music was everywhere—on radio, TV, movies and records. Even TV commercials used swing music. Little of this music was deep or great, but it reflected the rhythms and inflections of our American speech patterns. When I got interested in jazz at the age of 12, I was immediately drawn to the swing aspect of it. Gradually, I began to discern what was popular swing music and what was jazz. Some of this was along racial lines—Joe Williams was jazz, Frank Sinatra was pop—and some was on a deeper level of integrity and truthfulness—Bill Evans vs. Peter Nero.

I quickly found Duke Ellington and Count Basie as models for big bands. They were on TV and radio often. I started listening to jazz radio stations with hip New York disc jockeys like Billy Taylor, Ed Beach and Symphony Sid. When I went to a record store, I would look for the sides that I had heard on those shows. The first jazz record that I bought was Horace Silver and the Jazz Messengers. It was on the Blue Note label. I played that record so many times that I wore it out. If you want to know how to write for 2 horns, listen to that record… it's all there.

Aside from Horace, I had many other influences in small group jazz writing: Dizzy Gillespie, Thelonious Monk, Charles Mingus, Benny Golson, Thad Jones, Duke Pearson, Gigi Gryce, Rod Levitt, John Lewis, Gil Evans, Gerry Mulligan, and Bob Brookmeyer, as well as the great piano trios of Bill Evans, Erroll Garner, Sonny Clark, and Ahmad Jamal. I encourage you to listen to a wide variety of classic records and to analyze the arrangements.

In this book I will focus on how to write for quartet (1 horn plus rhythm section), quintet (2 horns), sextet (3 horns), and octet (5 horns). I will also discuss writing for 4 horns; this is covered in the 5-horn charts and analyses.

After you finish reading this book and have a grasp on basic arranging concepts, you may want to read my other two composing and arranging books: **Creative Jazz Composing and Arranging, Volume 1** (writing for big band) and **Creative Jazz Composing and Arranging, Volume 2: Writing for Singers**, which also discusses songwriting. They are a bit more advanced than this book, so I encourage you to read this one first. Also, writing for smaller groups gives you the ability to be economical, an invaluable skill when writing for larger ensembles. It will lead to leaner and more imaginative scores for big band and orchestra.

While I still write scores with pencil and paper before scribing them, many if not most of today's arrangers and composers write directly on the computer, with programs like Sibelius®, Finale® and Dorico®. There's no problem with using these programs, as long as you are telling *them* what to do, and not vice versa.

Sibelius® users: I encourage you to read my (mercifully brief) manual, **Streamlined Sibelius.**® The book and attached templates will help you create professional-looking scores and parts in a fraction of the time it takes without them. And I can't emphasize enough how much your music's appearance matters in how well it is played.

Well, all right then! Buckle your seatbelt. We are starting on a long journey of self-expression. I'm not going to have all the answers for you, but, hopefully, I'll get you to ask some good questions, and learn how to find the answers for yourself. The best education encourages you to be curious and teaches you how to teach yourself. Bon voyage.

Ever onward and upward,
David Berger

1. Definitions: Composing, Arranging, Orchestrating, Transcribing, Extracting

Before we start writing music, we need to define the various kinds of writing applied to music.

Composing: Writing a wholly original complete score, including all rhythms, pitches, harmonies, orchestration, and form. Any score by Mozart, Beethoven, or Stravinsky, for example, is considered a complete composition. We can also include compositions by jazz composers like Jelly Roll Morton, Duke Ellington, and Wynton Marsalis. Songwriters who compose the music to their songs are also called composers. This would include Richard Rodgers, Jerome Kern, Harold Arlen, and Harry Warren, as well as composer/lyricists like Cole Porter, Irving Berlin, and Steven Sondheim. These songwriters supplied lead sheets containing rhythm, melody, and chord symbols, leaving it to arrangers and orchestrators to complete their work.

Arranging: Taking previously existing musical material (like a song) and changing it by either: extending it beyond the original confines of the song form (usually 12, 16, or 32 bars), defining the pitches of the harmonies (sometimes adding, altering, or substituting harmonies), rephrasing the rhythms and/or pitches of the melody, creating rhythm section parts, and shaping the piece for a specific purpose (publication, concert, film, show, etc.). This can be very creative work depending on the composer, the arranger, and the situation.

Orchestrating: Assigning actual notes to specific instruments to complete a score. Sometimes this duty is assigned to the arranger. In this book, the terms arranger and orchestrator are used interchangeably.

Transcribing: Listening to a recorded piece of music and notating what you hear onto a score which, when played, will sound identical to the original recording. This type of work takes a trained ear, a good knowledge of arranging and orchestration, organizational skills and lots of patience.

Extracting: Also called copying, or engraving, of parts. Reproducing the individual instrument parts from a full score, so that each player has a separate part to read from. Although this appears to many people (musicians included) to be a mechanical task, a good copyist will create parts that look logical to the players and will reinforce what they are hearing and feeling, so that the part will be easily sight-readable.

In this book we will address the first three items in the list above: composing, arranging, and orchestrating. For transcribing, I recommend that you start with recordings of small groups and music that you can easily hear and carefully notate all the parts. Get your transcriptions played, and see how close you came. Gradually attempt more difficult recordings. (See my blog on transcribing at **https://www.suchsweetthundermusic.com/blogs/news/how-i-transcribe-jazz-recordings?page=2** .)

Copying scores and parts by hand is pretty much a thing of the past. I recommend that you use Sibelius,® unless you are already using Finale® or Dorico® successfully. I find Sibelius® easier to learn and more intuitive—but that's just me. For Sibelius® users: Once you have mastered the basics, I recommend that you read ***Streamlined Sibelius*** by Marc Schwartz, Christian Dancy, and myself, available from Such Sweet Thunder Books (www.SuchSweetThunderMusic.com).

This short book will teach you how to create professional looking parts and scores. We give you all the pre-sets, fonts, and rules, and make it as easy as possible for you. The musicians who play your music will thank you for making their job easier, and you will thank them for making your music sound better.

2. Basic Harmonization, Modulation and Creating a Lead Sheet

I'm going to assume that you know how to read music in the treble and bass clefs, and know a bit about harmony. If not, I suggest that you learn these things before continuing. There are a number of good books on music theory and on European classical harmony as well as jazz harmony. The more you know, the easier it will be for you to understand what I am talking about. I'll give you a brief overview of how harmony works. This is meant as a review, and to shore up any incomplete knowledge you may have.

Diatonic harmony is built on the major scale in any of the twelve keys. Since the invention of well-tempered tuning about 300 years ago, we can play music in any of the twelve keys, and all the pitches will relate to the others in the same way. So basically, if you play a song written in C and transpose all the notes down a major third to A♭, it will still sound like the same song. For the purposes of explaining tonal and chromatic harmony, I will stick to the key of C, but please realize that everything I show you can be transposed to the other eleven keys as well. Here is the major scale:

Example 2-1

Traditionally, triads are built in thirds on each step of the scale:

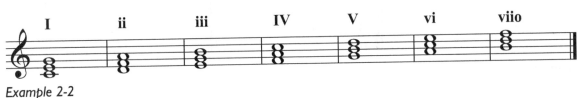

Example 2-2

In jazz we generally use 4-note chords:

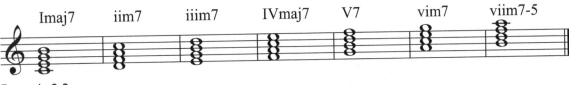

Example 2-3

Chord progressions mostly use the strongest root movements. Here they are in order of strong to weak:

CJCA III: Writing for Small Groups

- up a **perfect 4th** (same as down a **perfect 5th**)
- down a **minor 2nd**
- down a **3rd**
- up or down a **major 2nd**
- down a **perfect 5th** (up a **perfect 4th**)
- tritone (**diminished 5th** or **augmented 4th**)
- up a **3rd** (down a **6th**)

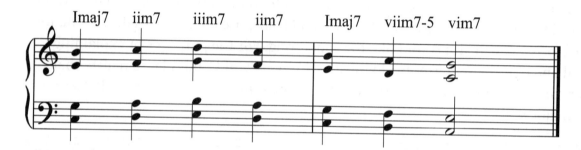

Example 2-4

For cadences, about 90% of the time we use an authentic cadence *(V to I)*. Sometimes a plagal cadence *(IV to I)* is used, for a churchy sound. In jazz we often like to use a ♭7 on the subdominant *(IV chord)* to make it more bluesy.

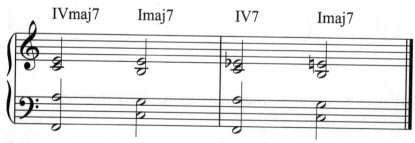

Example 2-5

HARMONIZATION

Here are a few common diatonic chord progressions:

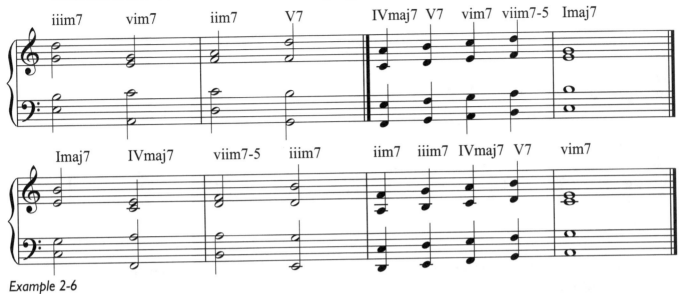

Example 2-6

We can also use diatonic harmony for music that is in a minor key, by starting on the 6th step of the scale (the relative minor):

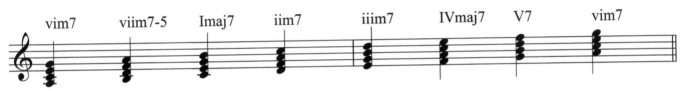

Example 2-7

In order to create a stronger authentic cadence in minor, we can raise the subtonic (7th step of the scale, or G) a half-step to the leading tone (G#). This gives us the harmonic minor scale:

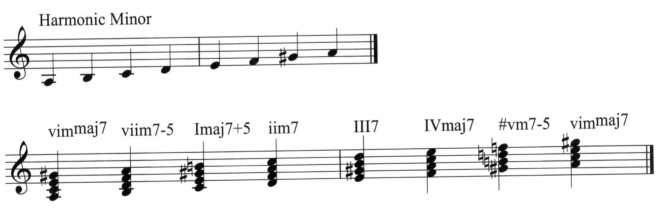

Example 2-8

We can go further and raise the 6th step as well, to create the ascending melodic minor scale:

Example 2-9

Here is a diatonic progression in A minor that uses the **natural**, **harmonic**, and **melodic minor chords**:

Example 2-10

Now let's transpose the three minor modes to C minor (the parallel minor of C major) and relabel the chords as if they are in C major:

HARMONIZATION

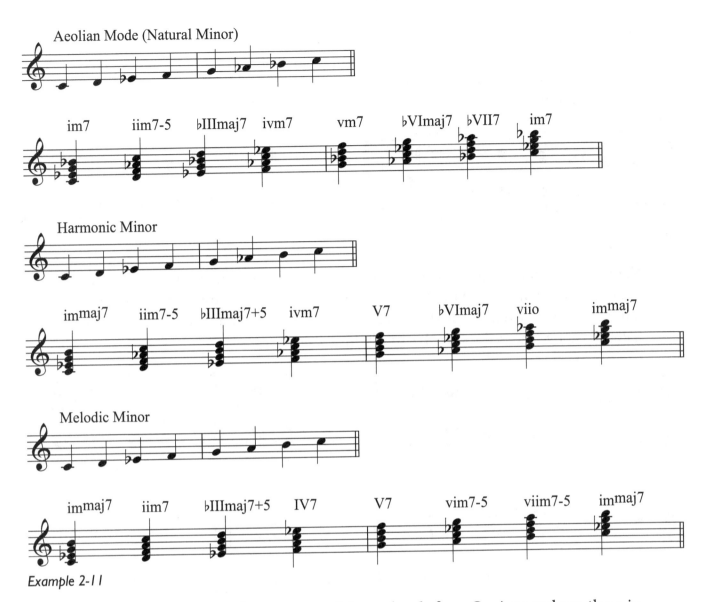

Example 2-11

For added color, we can borrow any of these chords from C minor and use them in C major progressions. For instance:

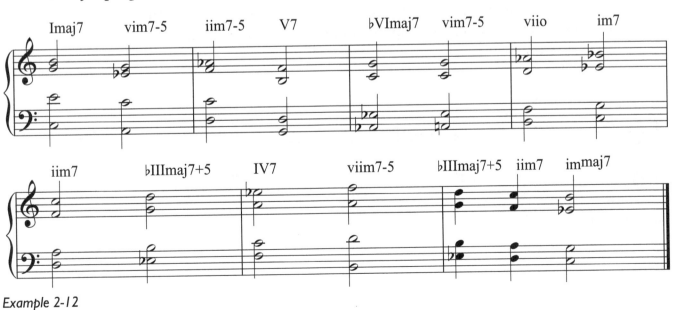

Example 2-12

Do you see how the *vii°* functions in C harmonic minor? It resolves smoothly up a half-step to the tonic Cm. We can use this diminished chord as a passing chord between two adjacent whole steps in the bass for either major or minor scales. In jazz, we traditionally add a major 6th to tonic and subdominant chords.

Example 2-13a

Note that the diminished passing chord works for all ascending progressions but does not work when resolving downward to a major chord, a tonic or subdominant minor *(i or iv)* or a dominant 7th chord. However, the half-diminished chord built a half-step above the *iv* does resolve nicely to the *ivm7*:

Example 2-13b

Similarly, we can precede any major or minor chord with a dominant 7th chord built a perfect 5th above (the dominant of the target chord). These are called secondary dominants:

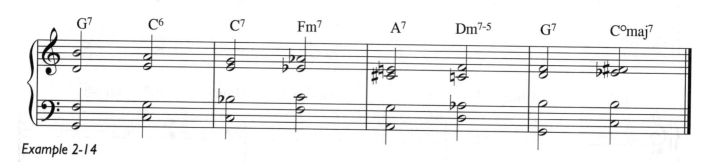

Example 2-14

HARMONIZATION

Furthermore, we can precede a secondary dominant with its own dominant (dominant 7th built a perfect 5th above) or its *ii* chord (m7 or m7-5):

Example 2-15

The common chord substitutions in European classical music are:
- Tonic subs: *iii* or *vi* for the *I* chord
- Dominant subs: *ii* or *vii°* for the *V* chord.

In jazz we frequently use the *iii* in place of the *I* chord to create a more melodic bass line and/or to avoid resolving to the tonic prematurely. Also, in jazz we frequently will use the *iim7* in place of the *V7*, but resolve to the *V7* before moving to another chord.

Example 2-16

The same is true of dominant substitutions. We use the *viim7-5* to resolve to the *iii* or *V/vi* (strong perfect 5th root movement) or to resolve down to a ♭VII7 or ♭vii° chord:

CJCA III: WRITING FOR SMALL GROUPS

Example 2-17

The ♭VII7 is often used as a substitute for the ivm6 chord, or it can follow a ivm7:

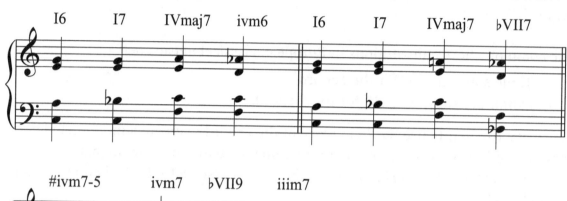

Example 2-18

Another common dominant substitution is the tritone sub. In the key of C, the dominant is G7. If you move a tritone (diminished 5th) away from G, you get D♭ or C#. Retaining the 3rd and 7th of the G7 chord (B and F), you'll notice that they are the same notes as the (7th and 3rd of D♭7), only in reverse position and with enharmonic spellings. In jazz we don't care about enharmonics much. We just like our parts to be as easy to read as possible.

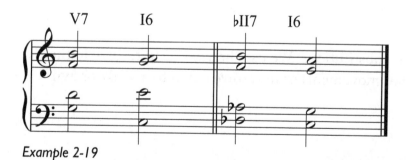

Example 2-19

One caveat: we normally avoid a ♭9 on the tritone sub. This is tricky to handle. I'll explain more about this later. For now, let's just avoid it.

Example 2-20

Harmonization

The basic chord changes reflect how the melody outlines the notes in the each of the chords. The next example is a lead sheet with the bass part written in (which sounds an octave lower), so you can see how the top and bottom feel complete (see *Example 2-21*). That's our meat and potatoes. When we add the inner parts of our harmonies, that's just the gravy. Always make sure that the melody and bass sound good together and have an interesting relationship.

I suggest that you sit at the piano and play just the melody and bass parts together. Remember to play the bass part an octave lower. I wrote it as if it were a string bass part. This avoids ledger lines, and will get you used to seeing bass parts the way bass players see them.

Do the two parts sound good together? Do they sound complete?

For folk songs like this, the chords are usually limited to *I, IV*, and *V*. This song is a bit more sophisticated in its use of the secondary dominant in measure **7** (G7 that resolves to C7 in bar **8**) and the leading tone dominant in bar **12** (A7 resolving to the subdominant B♭ in bar **13**). Leading tone dominant is a dominant 7th built on the root a half-step below the target chord.

Form

The form of this 16-bar song is *aa'bc* (four bars each). The first *a* section cadences on the tonic, while the second a section *(a')* ends in a semi-cadence (C7). Normally, we would expect the bridge (b section) to go F7-B♭ and then cycle back to F, so that the return of the a section could start on F (just like the previous **a** sections), but this song is more devious.

The *b* section stays on the dominant and resolves back to the tonic, which then goes down a 5th to the subdominant. We could use a tonic chord to harmonize the A melody note in bar **12**, but the surprise A7 is traditional and sounds so good.

I'VE BEEN WORKIN' ON THE RAILROAD

Example 2-21

The A7 resolves back up the half-step to the subdominant in bar **13** before going back to the tonic and then the traditional final cadence *V/V I64 V I*.

The last 4-bar section *(C)* starts on the subdominant (B♭) before resolving to the final tonic.

The harmonies are a bit rich for a folk song and the melody has an interesting shape and one chromatic note. But what holds this song together and makes it easy to learn is the repetitive rhythm—all of the four sections are basically identical rhythmically. This gives the song continuity, and allows us to explore more in the melodic and harmonic areas. Good songwriting is about balance.

Let's play the melody and bass again, now that we've analyzed it. Then play it adding 3rds and 7ths to the chords. If there is a 3rd or 7th in the melody or bass, do not repeat it in the inside voices. Next, add 5ths to the chords if the fifth does not appear in the melody or bass.

Root/5th on the bottoms of chords give stability and eliminate the necessity to double those notes higher up in the voicing. This leaves room for more colorful notes (3rds, 9ths, 6ths and 7ths) below the melody.

Now, let's have a little fun, and dress up the harmony a bit. We can make this traditional song sound more sophisticated by using chord substitution. Remember that re-harmonization is about dressing up the melody and giving it character—or in most cases, enhancing the character it already has. At no time do we want to go so far afield that we defile our original melody. Try this on for size (see *Example 2-22*):

Let's take a look at what's going on here. As I said, the melody stays the same. For now we are just re-harmonizing. I've written this on two staves with the bass notes written out in the bass clef so that you can see how I'm creating a complete and interesting 2-part arrangement between the melody and the bass.

Once these outside voices are established, the inner voices will easily fill themselves in. Notice how the bass has a good melody. One of the goals in arranging music is to give everyone a good melody to play. Another goal is to have each part relate in a pleasing and interesting way with all the other parts. I learned these principles from my study of Bach chorales as a child. This gives the music integrity and will make you friends with performers.

Scale-wise Patterns in the Bass

Although the roots of chords tend to move predominantly in 4ths and 5ths, bassists like to connect chords in stepwise motion much of the time. Sophisticated chord progressions balance these two. When you look at the intervals in the bass, you can see plenty of 4ths, 5th and 2nds. I'm particularly drawn to the scale-wise bass patterns:

Bars 1-3: Descends chromatically from C to B♭.

Bars 4-8: Starts descending diatonically from B♭ to E and then chromatically from E♭ to C.

Bar 5: Inserts the ascending diatonic line from F to A.

Bars 10-12: Descends diatonically from B♭ to E.

CJCA III: WRITING FOR SMALL GROUPS

I'VE BEEN WORKIN' ON THE RAILROAD

Example 2-22

Bars 13-14: Ascends chromatically from B♭ to C.

Bars 14-16: Descends diatonically C to A, then chromatically from A♭ to G and diatonically to F.

Bars 15-16: Interrupts the previous pattern first with a descending half-step (D♭ to C), then an ascending half-step (E to F), and finally an ascending 4th (F to B♭) and an ascending 5th (B♭ to F).

HARMONIZATION

Tapping into our Subconscious Minds

Note how the final four bars sum up all the bass movement of the previous 12 bars. This is very satisfying. In case you are thinking, "How does he think of all this stuff?", the truth is that, until I started analyzing the bass part in writing this chapter, I had no idea any of this was going on. I just wrote a bass line that interacted with the melody that sounds pleasing to me. The underlying structure came from my subconscious mind, which has been storing up harmonies since I was an infant.

The Nature of Genius

About 30 years ago Wynton Marsalis told me about a woman he knew who had the ability to understand how vastly different information was related. No one else could see these relationships. He defined this ability as genius. I think there may be a little bit more to genius, but certainly this has to be one important element.

In music there are composers, arrangers, and players who have taken elements of one style or genre and infused into another in an integral way. Integral is the key word here. Think of Ray Charles, who brought Gospel and country music into jazz. Duke Ellington expressed extra-musical ideas in his music, from the sounds of trains to interpersonal relationships, to the underpinnings of culture.

Artists who dare to do these things take great risks, but may enjoy great success. (And then there are artists like Vincent van Gogh, who was just too far ahead of his time to be appreciated.)

Play the melody and bass together. Interesting? Granted, it's a bit sophisticated for your old-time railroad workers to sing, but it could make a fun choir arrangement or a soundtrack for a documentary on the Twentieth Century Limited. I chose this song because I assume everyone knows it, and it's a great melody that will support all kind of reharmonization—which is what I'm demonstrating in this book.

Diatonic Passing Chords

We can dress up measure **1** with a *ii V* to relieve the monotony of six beats of the tonic. The Gm7 with a C in the bass is a C7sus4 and accommodates the F in the melody. Bar **2** starts with an Fmaj7 rather than F triad or F6. The E on the maj7 creates a nice inner line, F E D#.

Harmony is the artificial freezing of a moment and labeling the vertical sounds that are created by the coincidence of all the melodies.

Tritone Substitution

The B7-5 is the tritone sub for F7. Since we are going to B♭ in bar **3**, we can approach it from its dominant (F7). Because there is an F in the melody, I would rather not have an F in the bass—I like to avoid too much agreement between the melody and bass until the final resolution.

Another thing I like about this B7 is the ♭5 in the melody. It's interesting to use 9ths, 11ths, 13ths and their alterations in the melody. At the same time, we want our melodies to be singable, which in many cases means diatonic. There is only one accidental in this whole section, (the F# in bar **9**).

Re-harmonizing diatonic melodies with chromatic chords can make a simple melody sound fresh and modern.

The Chord of Despair

We can add more story to the subdominant (B♭ chord) in bar **4** by subtly sliding the 3rd down a half-step to form a B♭m6. So often the *IV* moves to the *ivm*. The ♭*VII7* (E♭7) is often used as a substitute for the *ivm*, or sometimes B♭ B♭m7 E♭7, depending on the melody, the amount of movement. the desired harmonic rhythm, and the level of sophistication represented in the piece.

The *ivm* chord is the chord of despair. This occurs when the lyric is "all the live-long day." The *ivm* gives this phrase weight. I can feel my shoulders slumping with exhaustion.

On the other hand, using a ♭*VII7* (E♭7) or building a *ii V* (B♭7 E♭7) sounds sophisticated rather than sorrowful, and thus might not be as good a choice as the B♭m6.

More Diatonic Progressions

Instead of remaining on the tonic (F) chord for bars **4-6**, we could use parallel diatonic chords—just walking down and up the major scale: *I IV iii ii, I ii iii*.

Looking Ahead and Working Backwards

If we look ahead to the G7 *(V/V)* in bar **7**, we can work backwards from there and see where it takes us. The F#° resolving upwards by half-step is the strongest diminished progression. Diminished chords can function as rootless dominant 7-9 chords. So, in this case, the F#° is like a D7-9 resolving up a fourth to G7 *(V/ii V/V)*. Any chord can be preceded by its dominant. The two bass motions are down a perfect 5th (up a perfect 4th), down a half-step, or up a half-step.

Interupting a Resolution

In this case, the F#° interrupts the Dm7, resolving to the G7. Although the root movement is down a 5th (D down to G), the Dm7 is a diatonic chord in F major *(vi)* and not a dominant approach to the G7. The F#° introduces the F# leading tone to the G. It's merely a passing chord, and could be eliminated without disturbing anything, but if we use it, it adds a moment of color, especially with the E♭ in it—a blue note in the key of F).

HARMONIZATION

Substitute Dominants

The E♭7 is a dominant 7th that resolves down a half-step to the Dm7. That is reason enough for why it sounds good, but it is also the tritone sub of A7, which is the dominant of Dm. Similarly, E7 precedes the E♭7. The E7 was added as an afterthought. It adds a lot of color with the melody note, G, being the +9 of the E7, but I could have left the Am7 E♭7 Dm7 alone. The main thrust of the progression is Am7 Dm7, with the E♭7 (or E7 E♭7) as interruptions. Again, the E♭ in the bass is a blue note in the key of F.

More About Interruptions

I'm not concerned with the relationship of the lead-in to the interruption (Dm7 F#°, Am7 E7, or Am7 E♭7) if the interruption gets us to our goal.

In bar **8**, instead of going directly to C7 on the downbeat, we can delay it by using the dominant 7th a half-step above (D♭7) and then resolving to the C7. This works out particularly nicely since the melody note, G, is the ♭5 of the D♭7. This D♭7 can be approached from a half-step above, but D7 doesn't sound good because the G in the melody creates a minor 9th interval with the 3rd of the chord (F#). This led me to the diatonic *vi* chord, Dm7, where the G is the 11th of the chord. I don't care about the relationship of Dm7 and the previous G7. Dm7 interrupts and starts us on a new journey back to the tonic.

Keeping the Original Bass Line

I'm going to keep the original bass line for bar **9** and the downbeat of bar **10**. Instead of starting bar **9** on C7 with the 5th in the bass, I'm building a Gm7 on the G bass note and then resolving to the C7 and F *(ii V I)*. I'm not thrilled about the unison between the melody and bass on the downbeats of these two measures, but it's a very strong progression and the +11 and 13 on the C7 are very rich.

Traditional Subs

The traditional substitutes for the tonic are the *iii* and the *vi*. We hear both in bar **10**. The *iii* (Am7) is preceded from a step above—the *iv* chord (B♭maj7), thus creating *I IV iii vi* and resolving to Gm7 *(ii)* —all diatonic 7th chords moving by step, or around the circle of 5ths.

The Gm7 on the downbeat of bar **11** is a *ii* subbing for the *IV* and avoiding the melody-bass unison that the original B♭ bass note would have given us. I could stay on the Gm7 for the entire bar, but the lyric says, "Rise up," so it's nice to have the bass jump up at that moment. I could have put a rest on beat 2, but I was hearing the second beat as a chromatic chord. The B♭ melody becomes the 13th of a D♭7. The D♭ is sandwiched between two G's.

Holding Over a Chromatic Pitch

Although the melody and bass line starting on beat 3 of bar **11** is diatonic, inside parts contain chromatics. The D♭ that was in the bass on beat 2 of bar **11** moves to an inside part on the next beat, slightly changing the Gm7 to Gm7-5. The bass then walks down the scale from G to E for the Em7-5 (the diatonic vii⁰ chord) and then resolves to the A7 (*V/vi* or leading tone dominant to *IV*). The A7 has the interesting C# and could also contain a ♭9 (the diatonic pitch B♭).

A Touch of Gospel

Bars **13-14** are a typical example of the *IV #iv⁰ I64* progression that is so common in Gospel music. The passing diminished resolves up by half-step to the second inversion of the tonic F chord. We could proceed to a Dm7 or D7+9, but I like the descending scale in the bass that moves in contrary motion to the melody in bar **14**.

Ornamentation

Bars **15-16** are basically *ii V I* (Gm7 C7 F). I preceded the C9 with a D♭9 (chromatic approach/chromatic planing from a half-step above in parallel motion with the melody) and preceded the F with a dominant 7th a half-step below in contrary motion to the melody. I want this approach to the final tonic to be special. The melody note G makes the +9 on the E7, which gives us a feeling of the blues.

Rather than just hang on the tonic F for the final bar, I threw in the *ivm7* (B♭m7) as a sandwich chord. I like how the D♭ resolves to the D♮ of the F6 and the A♭ resolves to the A♮. If we add a quarter note alto line C D♭ D♮ and a tenor line A A♭ A♮, we could have bottom three voices sing, "Blow your horn!" in answer to the soprano.

Inverted Pedal Point

Or we could continue downward from the E7+9 to E♭69 and then upward E6 F6. The F whole note makes the 9th on the E♭6 and the root on the F6. It also makes the unusual ♭9 on the E6. This works because the tonic F is held out in the melody while the chords move underneath it. We call this inverted pedal point. The most common pedal point is where the *bass* note stays the same or is repeated while the *other* voices move. Pedal point can also occur on top or in the middle of voicings.

[Play the entire song with the re-harmonization. Does it hang together? Feel balanced? Are you satisfied at the end?]

3. Four-Part Harmony

Jazz harmony is based on four notes per chord. In fact, all of the chords we commonly use in jazz can be reduced to four parts: 1, 3, 5, 7 or 1, 3, 5, 6 with alterations. Here are the six chord types:

Example 3-1

Major Chords: Traditionally, in jazz, when we have a major triad, if we wish to add a fourth note, we add the 6th. The major 6th chord expresses joy and wonder. It just makes us feel happy and optimistic.

Minor Chords: Similarly, when we have a minor triad, we can add the major 6th. Minor triads feel somewhat sad, but due to the tritone between the 3rd and 6th, minor chords with a minor 6th express hopelessness or despair.

Minor Seventh Chords: Minor sevenths are bland. I call them the middle-class chord: Life is okay—I'm not rich, but I make a living.

Minor Seventh Flat Five or Half-diminished Chords: These chords pull at your heartstrings. They are unstable and must resolve. Their instability results from the tritone between the root and the ♭5.

Diminished Seventh Chords (Diminished Chords): Melodramatic. In silent movies, when the villain would tie the ingenue to the railroad tracks, this is the chord the organist would play. These chords contain two tritones, which makes them very unstable. The tritones occur between the root and the ♭5, and between the minor 3rd and the diminished 7th. They beg to be resolved.

Dominant Seventh Chords: This is the most frequently used chord in jazz. The ♭7 creates a tritone with the 3rd of the chord and therefore is unstable. Although in European classical music dominant 7ths must resolve, in jazz we frequently use dominant 7th chords as major chords, with tonic and subdominant functions. This is a typical blues sound. In fact, we can substitute a dominant 7th structure for any of the other five sonorities. Of course, we want to use this option judiciously. If we overdo it, our music can become predictable, even one-dimensional.

(continued)

CJCA III: Writing for Small Groups

Voicings

Voicings are the choice of pitches and their vertical spacings. In the above musical example, you will notice that each chord is built up in 3rds. All four notes are different and are within the octave. This is called block harmony, 4-part close, or 4-way close. In the 1920s, jazz started the transition from 3-part triadic harmonies to 4-part chords. Duke Ellington led the way. His use of block chord voicings in the horns added richness to his orchestrations.

Inversions

In the musical examples above, I spelled each chord in root position. These voicings are used to thicken the melody line. They do not include the bassist, who is responsible for the roots of the chords on the bottom. Because of the bassist, we can invert all of these voicings without changing the inversion of the chord itself, so that any of the four notes can be on the bottom, middle, or top.

Example 3-2

Let's voice out this melody in 4-part close harmony:

Example 3-3

The first thing we need to do is to add 6ths to the major and tonic minor chords:

Example 3-4

There are three syncopations in this short fragment. The first note occurs on the *and*-of-1. It gets voiced with the C6 of the previous beat. The other two syncopations (the F# on the *and*-of-4 of the first bar and the G on the *and*-of-4 of the second bar both anticipate the harmonies that the rhythm section will play on the next beat. These anticipations are voiced with the upcoming beat, as such:

Example 3-5

This works out great, as long as all the melody notes are in the chords. But what if a melody note is not in the chord?

Example 3-6

Voicing from the top down, we can omit the next lower chord tone:

Example 3-7

Similarly, we often avoid roots on the inside of our voicings, since the bassist covers them. Bass notes are very strong. Doubling them inside can ground the voicing too much. It's a question of balance and style. To avoid over-grounding, we can use 9ths in place of the roots, and in the case of dominants (V7) in minor keys, we often use a -9 or a +9:

Example 3-8

Similarly, in minor, we often alter the 5th of the dominant, raising it a half-step. So in Cm, we might use a G7+5 or, in conjunction with an altered 9th, G7-9+5 or G7+9+5.

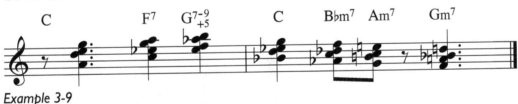

Example 3-9

It is common practice to borrow chords from the parallel minor to use in the major, so in C major, we might also use an altered G7 chord (e.g. G7-9+5).

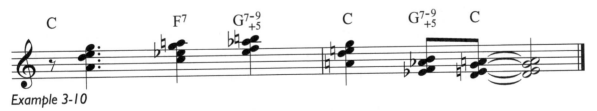

Example 3-10

Tension Chart

A major consideration in writing music is tension and release. This helps to create the ebb and flow in music. In jazz, there are traditional tensions that can substitute for chord tones by replacing the next lower chord tone. For instance, if you choose to use a major 7th on a major or minor chord, omit the 6th, or if you choose to use an 11th on a m7-5 chord, omit the 3rd. The following is a chart of the most common tensions:

Example 3-11

Depending on the situation, alterations are frequently used on dominant 7ths: + or -5 and + or − 9. Natural 11ths are usually treated as sus4s. They omit the 3rd. Natural 11ths include the 3rds; avoid them for now. We will discuss them later.

Open Voicings

There are four varieties of open voicings:

Drop 2: Start with a block voicing and drop the second voice from the top down an octave. This will leave a 4th or 5th between the new top two voices. You may consider replacing the new second voice with a tension. This is optional and will depend on the amount of dissonance desired, voice leading in that part, and how that part relates to the other notes in the voicing.

This is the most common semi-open voicing, and is most useful when voicing chords for dissimilar instruments—for example, three trumpets and one trombone; or two alto saxes, a tenor and a bari; or one alto, two tenors, and a bari.

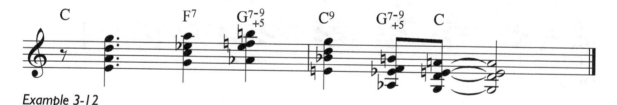

Example 3-12

Drop 3: Start with a block voicing and drop the third voice from the top down an octave. This will leave a 4th or 5th between the new second and third voices. You may consider replacing the new third voice with a tension. This is optional, and will depend on the amount of dissonance desired, voice leading in that part, and how that part relates to the other notes in the voicing.

Drop 3 isn't used that often, but it can be effective in emphasizing the relationship between the top two voices, for instance, major 2nds or 3rds.

4-PART HARMONY

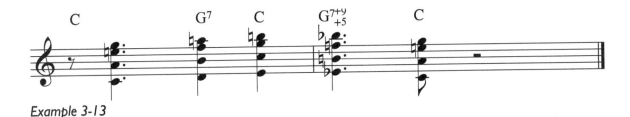

Example 3-13

Drop 2 & 4: Start with a block voicing and drop the second and fourth voice from the top down an octave. This will leave a 4th or 5th between the new top two voices. You may consider replacing the new second voice with a tension. This is optional and will depend on the amount of dissonance desired, voice leading in that part, and how that part relates to the other notes in the voicing. The point of Drop 2 & 4 is to achieve an effective open voicing. This works great for two trumpets and two trombones, or four saxes.

Example 3-14

Note: Don't be afraid to use open voicings. They sound better in horns (and strings) than you think they will. The greater the distance between the top and bottom notes of your voicing, the greater the weight.

Chorale Voicings: The above voicings are created by starting with the top voice and proceeding downwards. This works great for thickening a melodic line, hence Ray Wright's term, "thickened line" voicings. Sometimes we like more bottom on the sound. We can achieve this by putting a root in the fourth voice. We call this chorale voicing, as in the chorales that Bach wrote 350 years ago. Typical chorale voicings from the bottom up are: 1, 5, 3, 6; 1, 7, 3, 5; 1, 3 (a 10th above the root), 6, 5. It is common to replace the 6th with the major 7th. Also once the root, 3rd and 7th are established in the lower three parts, you may want to replace the 5th with the 9th. These same spacings may be used for the other five chord types as well.

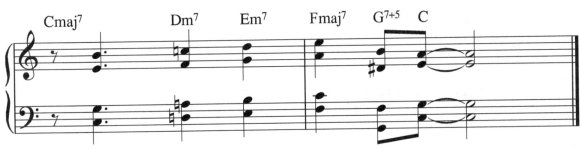

Example 3-15

23

Voicings Determined by Intervallic Relationships

When you are looking for something special, you might try these: voicings of like intervals, i.e., all 4ths or all 5ths. This was commonplace in the 1960s.

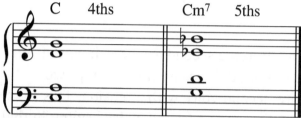

Example 3-16

Symmetrical voicings are also very effective: the interval between the top two voices is also the interval between the bottom two. The dissonant Z-cell was popularized by Béla Bartók and entered the jazz vocabulary a few decades later in the 1960s. It contains two tritones a half-step apart, as well as two perfect 4ths a half-step apart.

Example 3-17

Mirror inversions are also useful. This is where the interval between the bottom two voices is the inversion of the interval between the top two.

Example 3-18

Cluster voicings (two or more consecutive 2nds) can give you a foil against the sound of open voicings.

Example 3-19

4-PART HARMONY

Passing Chords

We frequently employ passing chords to avoid unwanted repeated notes and create better melodies for the inside parts. There are four basic techniques, each of which could be used exclusively for an entire passage or combined with one or more of the other techniques. When creating passing chords, we generally work backwards from the target chord. In many or even most cases, we don't inform the rhythm section of the passing chords.

Chromatic: If the melody moves by half-step, working backwards, move all four parts chromatically in the same directions.

Example 3-20

Diminished: Build a diminished chord from the top down.

Example 3-21

Dominant: Working backwards, treat the target chord as a tonic and create a dominant of that target chord.

Example 3-22

Diatonic: If the melody moves diatonically (stepwise within a key), working backwards, move all the voices in stepwise fashion diatonically in the same direction.

Example 3-23

That's about it for 4-note voicings for now. We will discuss these techniques as well as 2-, 3- and 5-note voicings in detail in later chapters.

4. Mary's A Grand Old Name
Quartet Arrangement (1 Horn)

When I was growing up in the 1950s, we didn't have the Internet, but we did have television. Our TV screen was about the size of my current laptop. The picture was in black and white, but I was fortunate—I lived just outside New York City, so we got good reception of the eight New York stations. Much of the country was lucky if they got three stations.

There were three networks: CBS, NBC, and ABC. The other stations were local and presented low-budget programming like wrestling, baseball, children's shows such as *Howdy Doody*, old syndicated sitcoms like *Amos 'n' Andy*, *The Life of Riley*, and *I Love Lucy*, and old movies from the 1930s and '40s. On channel 9 (WOR), there was *Million Dollar Movie*. They showed the same movie every day for an entire week, twice or even three times a day. Since we didn't have any way to record shows, we had to watch everything in real time, and catch it while it was being aired.

My brothers and I loved *King Kong* (the uncut original 1933 version) and couldn't get enough of it. That got me into the habit of watching *Million Dollar Movie*. When I found a movie I liked, I would watch it several times before eagerly awaiting its return a year or two later. I pretty much gave every genre a chance.

There were Westerns, war movies, dramas—all kinds of stuff. One day I discovered musicals. I remember one with Al Jolson singing *About A Quarter To Nine*, corny dated stuff, but my favorite old musical was *Yankee Doodle Dandy*, a biopic about songwriter/vaudeville song and dance man George M. Cohan. I don't know why, but I loved this movie—maybe because it starred James Cagney. I knew Cagney as a tough guy from his many great gangster roles. But he could sing, and was a terrific dancer. I watched *Yankee Doodle Dandy* many times and then again, when it returned every couple of years. I learned all the songs in it.

The movie was made in 1942, the year George Cohan died, but most of the action took place in the early 1900s. Cohan was a prolific Tin Pan Alley songwriter with more than 300 songs to his credit. Between 1904 and 1920 he produced and created over 50 Broadway plays, musicals and revues. At times he had as many as five shows running at the same time on Broadway, and his musicals gave birth to such standards as *You're a Grand Old Flag*, *Forty-Five Minutes from Broadway*, *Mary's A Grand Old Name*, *The Yankee Doodle Boy*, *Harrigan*, and *Over There*. When I grew up, everyone knew all these songs, and they were all in that movie.

Granted, Cohan's songs (most of which are about 100 years old) sound dated if you play them as they were performed originally. But they have such strong melodies and construction that they retain their quaint appeal. Here is **Mary's A Grand Old Name** in its original form:

MARY'S A GRAND OLD NAME

George M. Cohan

Example 4-1 *Mary's A Grand Old Name* lead sheet with lyrics

Song Form

When we omit the verse, the 16-bar form of this song is *abac* (4 measures per section). Short and sweet. In the American Songbook we normally see 32-bar forms with 8-bar sections, but occasionally 16 or 64-bar forms creep into the repertoire. Usually the shorter forms are played slowly or at medium tempo, and the 64-bar forms are traditionally played in 2 at fast tempos. The idea is that, in general, one chorus should take about a minute to perform.

Learn the Lyrics

I always learn the lyrics to songs that I arrange. The words convey the spirit of the song, and how the melody relates to the rhythms and inflections of how we speak. When I write an instrumental arrangement, I don't focus as much on the specifics of the lyrics as I would if someone were singing them. However, I always keep the words in my subconscious and forever link them with the melody. Remember that the lyrics are your biggest clue as to what the song is about.

Finding an Angle

I've always liked **Mary's A Grand Old Name**, and recently had an idea to give it a more modern, relaxed mainstream jazz treatment. First, I played it a half-dozen times on the piano. Each time I discovered new rhythms and harmonies that gradually built on the ones I had played before. Eventually I arrived at my concept of this song—my point of view. My process is to keep playing it (or singing it in my head) until I find an angle, so the arrangement feels like my song and not an external generic treatment of someone else's music. Now, and only now, am I ready to commit pencil to paper.

The two motifs that intrigue me about this melody are:

The ascending chromatics in measures **7** and **13**. Bar **7** goes *re, ri, mi*, and bar **13** is *sol, si, la*. The rest of the tune is diatonic.

The diatonic scale-wise movement is first hinted at in measure **3**, but fleshed out in bars **5-6** and then in bar **14**.

Both motifs occur in dramatic places in the melody. The E's in bars **13** and **14** are the highest note (climax) of the song. Since both the ascending chromatic and diatonic movement attract me, I'm going to use those concepts in my accompaniment to give the arrangement integrity; to make the foreground and background inseparable, and give everyone something important to do.

Let Your Subconscious Mind do the Work

Just to be clear, I was completely unaware of these structural details when I wrote this chart—I wasn't thinking about any of this consciously. I was just writing what sounded good to me. Now, months later, I am analyzing what I did. In order to explain it, I see things that my subconscious mind was supplying unbeknownst to my conscious thinking. As I've said before, my subconscious mind drew on a lifetime of hearing and playing music, and put these pieces of the puzzle together in an interesting way. Once the music was down on paper, I consciously asked myself, "Does it sound good?" and "Is there something I should change to make it sound better and make more sensible, without destroying the inspiration?" And finally, "Is it compelling? Does it tell a story?"

Don't Mess with the Identity of the Song

In this case I kept the original Cohan melody mostly in place, just adding a few auxiliary pitches to dress it up. Mostly I changed the rhythms so that they would be more conversational—less stiff and predictable. Keep in mind that what made all the great songs in the American Songbook great was their melodies and words. The rhythms and harmonies are less identifiable. In fact, if we keep the words and melodies, and create our own rhythms and harmonies, listeners will still recognize the songs, and we can treat them to new, personalized arrangements that will become our own music.

Honor the Song

Sometimes I hear arrangements that violate the original song. The arranger doesn't honor the essence of the original and goes too far—destroying its charm. Bob Brookmeyer called arranging "dressing up the baby." Referring to some of his later work, he said that he went as far as to remove the baby's arms, legs, and head, and reassemble them in a more abstract way. I always learn the original rhythms and harmonies. Once I know them, I am free to respectfully play with them.

Example 4-2

Notice the liberal use of syncopations. These give the music forward motion and add instability, rhythmic diversity, and surprise, while helping to establish this arrangement as jazz. I've added a few notes here and there to make the melody more conversational. Because of the chromatic and diatonic motifs present in the original melody, I'm going to follow suit and add more of those.

The four repeated Ds in bar **6** serve both as relief from the obvious ascending line and as dominant tonal anchors. The lower neighbor C# on beat 4 previews the chromatics of the next measure. Similarly, the G on the *and*-of-beat 1 in bar **13** is a tonic anchor. I added the A and B in bar **15** to dress up the standard *la, ti, do* cadence. The added A and B refer to the ascending diatonic scheme begun in bar **3** and tie up the package nicely.

Melody-bass Relationship

My next step was to create an accompanying bass part that would give the trumpet melody more of the character that I'm hinting at. Note that the bass is always written an octave above where it sounds. The bass part will consist mainly of the roots of the chords; but also, if played by itself, will be a convincing melodic line. As you can see, in order to establish two independent melodies, I've avoided unisons between the trumpet and the bass, with the following exceptions:

Second beat of bar **A6**. The independence is not compromised because of the **contrary motion** between the two parts. Omitting the repeated ghosted dominant pedals (D's), the trumpet ascends (F#, G, A), while the bass descends (A, G, F#).

Example 4-3 Melody-bass relationship

On the *and*-of-3 in bar **A8**, the dominant (D) is purposely sounded in the bass to **signal the return** to the *a* section. The trumpet repeats the dominant note, but then ascends up a tonic triad to set up the tonic on the following measure.

On the **final tonic** G in bar **B8,** the bass delays, but finally agrees. After I know the melody-bass relationship, I put in the chord symbols. Very often the melody note will determine the chord quality. Melodies that rely heavily on 9ths, 11ths, 13ths, and their alterations are appealing to me. They set up complex relationships with the bass.

[Play the melody and bass parts together on the piano. They sound complete, right? This is our meat and potatoes. Any harmony notes that are added in other horns or by the pianist will just be gravy. Good melody-bass relationship is an essential part of all great music. It is the foundation upon which we build our melodic/harmonic structure.]

Roots and Inversions

The bass note is usually the root of the chord, but occasionally the chord can be an inversion as on the downbeat of bar **A6**. In most cases inversions are used to create stepwise motion in the bass. In bar **A6** the bass descends scale-wise while the melody ascends diatonically in contrary motion.

The roots of chords are mostly connected by stepwise motion (chromatic or diatonic) as in bars **A2-3**. Sometimes we can jump octaves (**A5** and **B5**). It is also strong to alternate roots and 5ths. We can also arpeggiate the chords using triads, 6th chords or 7th chords. Because the harmonic rhythm is mostly two beats per chord, there isn't much opportunity for arpeggios.

Living in the Subconscious Mind

Also, because of the chromatic and diatonic motifs mentioned above, I've limited the bass line to those same melodic patterns to give the chart unity. Again, this was not a conscious decision, but just what sounded good to me and satisfied my sense of order. I relied on my subconscious mind to create the music, then I did a bit of tidying up with my conscious, logical, linear mind after the initial ideas were on the page. I try to limit the use of my conscious mind, and let the music sing itself. Any use of my logical, conscious mind is purely to get me back to my subconscious or to tie up loose ends. The music should always be logical—but not *too* logical. As in our dreams, our subconscious is complicated and devious. Great music sounds surprising and inevitable at the same time.

Chord Qualities

Notice that many, if not most, of the melody notes suggest upper tensions of the chords. For example, the first melody note (D) is the 13th of the F7 chord. I like these complex melody-bass relationships. There are 60 melody notes in **A** and **B**. 31

are tensions (above the 7th of the chord) and 29 are 1, 3, 5, 6 or 7. I didn't plan this. This is just what sounded good and balanced to me. Every arrangement has different proportions depending on the character of the song and the arrangement.

Since all but one of the bass notes is the root of the chord, I can deduce which function each melody note has in each chord. In some cases I have two or more choices. For instance, the second melody note (B) is the 5th of an E chord. Being in the key of G, most likely that would be a diatonic chord (Em7) or a secondary dominant (E7). In this situation, the E7 sounds better to my ear. The diatonic Em7 sounds a bit bland. The G# in the E7 adds a little spice. I feel there should be more tension in this spot than the diatonic Em7 gives us.

Balancing tension and release is a primary concern in writing music.

In general, I use diatonic chords whenever I can. Of the 43 chords in **A** and **B**, 15 are diatonic. There are 19 chords built on chromatic bass notes, so, the remaining 9 chords that are built on diatonic bass notes use non-diatonic chords like the above-mentioned E7 in **A1**. Other such chords are the C7 chords (I like using the dominant 7th sonority on *IV* chords—it feels like the blues and also gives an extra pull to the *iii* chord that follows it), Gm6 (really a rootless C9 in 2nd inversion), F#m7 rather than F#m7-5—I like the chromaticism of the C# (the natural 5th of the F#m7) following the Gm6, and the penultimate F# major triad that resolves chromatically up to the tonic G triad.

I used dominant 7th chords for the chromatic bass notes with two exceptions: the Bb° in **A5** and the C#m7-5 in **B4**. Both of these chords were suggested by the relationship of the melody notes to the bass.

Picking the Key for the Arrangement

To pick which key to write your arrangement in, first decide who will play the melody, and then pick the key in which that instrument or singer sounds best for the notes of that tune.

In the case of **Mary** (see *Score* and pp. 36-41), I chose the key of G because it puts the trumpet in his middle register; his lowest note is concert C# just above middle C, and his highest note is E a 10th above. I'm looking for a relaxed *mf* groove. I don't want the trumpet to be screaming above the staff, nor do I want him to be below the staff, where he sounds tubby and can't project. There are times when those extreme registers are just what you want, but this isn't one of them. In general, the more horns we have in the ensemble, the higher we write the trumpet.

Trumpet-Bass Relationship

After the trumpet part, I write the bass part. Like the trumpet, I mostly keep the bass in the staff. Remember, the bass sounds an octave lower than written. The overall principle in play with the relationship between the lead melody part (trumpet in this case) and the bass is that the greater the distance between them, the bigger the sound; conversely, the shorter the distance, the more intimate the sound. Therefore, quieter passages necessitate a lower trumpet part and a higher bass part, and loud passages will have the trumpet higher in his range and the bass near the bottom of the bass clef.

Carefully consider where you want contrary motion, parallel motion, or oblique motion between these two instruments. **Contrary motion** has the two parts moving in opposite directions and creates a complex texture emphasizing the independence of the parts. **Parallel motion** conveys unity, and if there are parallel octaves or fifths, it feels more like one instrument than two. Independence is lost.

Oblique motion is where one voice stays on the same pitch while the other moves. This is an often overlooked, but very effective technique. This has the feeling of pedal point, which in most cases has the bass holding onto his pitch, while the other voices move. The opposite is also quite effective—inverted pedal point, where the top voice stays the same while the lower voice or voices move.

Dynamics, Accents, Longs and Shorts

Someone once asked Duke Ellington, "How much information do you give the bass player?" To which he answered, "As little as possible." He never wrote a drum part or piano part (*he* played the piano, and had a superb memory). His copyist constructed the guitar parts until 1948, when his guitarist, Fred Guy, left the band. He was never replaced. Ellington wanted his rhythm section to function like the rhythm section in a small group—improvising their own parts. Of course, he had a working band. They rehearsed new pieces and then played them every night—50 weeks per year. Nowadays, we rarely have that luxury.

Also, you'll never see a meter signature, dynamic marking, accent, or long or short notations in Ellington's music. When his copyist passed out the parts, the music belonged to the players. Their interpretation was welcomed. After counting off the tempo, Ellington inserted himself only when necessary. He always liked to see what everyone else had in mind. As much as possible, I like to carry on that approach. With school bands, this may not work so well, since the musicians don't have a lot of experience, but with professionals, I like them to bring their individual styles to the table. Then it is my job to get us all to agree on an interpretation.

I always include meter signatures—this is standard procedure. Although I like my music played with a variety of dynamics, I just notate the general volume and any specific stylistic spots that are out of the norm, like *subito p*. I encourage interpretation from the players. I use the traditional swing notation of quarter notes being played short, unless marked otherwise. Sometimes they could go either way, and I will leave that up to the players. Eighth notes are generally played legato except when followed by a rest, when they are short.

Some arrangers write a dynamic and a long or short and an accent on every single note. In my experience, this is too much information for players to assimilate on the spot. The result is that nobody reads any of those things, and they just play everything loud, long and with no accents—BORING! We like variety and surprise. If you over-notate, and give the players too much instructions, they might look for ways to be creative, such as playing their parts up an octave.

Rhythmic Independence

Notice how the trumpet and bass mostly have different rhythms. They are designed to complement each other and keeping things moving and interesting. Sometimes it's effective to give the piano and drums the same rhythms as the bass.

Transposing the Score

Let's look at letters **A** and **B** in the transposed score (see *Score* pp. 2-3/pp. 37-38). When I was growing up, all professional scores were transposed, so that the conductor saw the parts just as the players saw them. I learned to write this way. The summer before my senior year of high school, I went to the Berklee School of Music (now Berklee College of Music). They had us write our scores in Concert. When I returned to high school in September, my band director said to me, "I know you are not thinking about this now, but one day, you will have a copyist to copy your parts, and if you don't transpose the score, you'll have to pay him 50% extra. Go back to writing transposed scores. One day you'll thank me. I just saved you a million dollars."

With Finale® and Sibelius®, transposing isn't a big deal, but I still like to see all players' parts exactly as they see them. This helps me make them comfortable and happy. If they like playing my music, they will try hard to make it sound good and will want to play with me again. Some players have even come to like me, and we have become friends.

Writing for Piano

In letters **A** and **B**, there was no need to write out specific pitches for the pianist. I assume that s/he has experience playing in jazz bands and knows:

- How to interpret standard chord notation.

- How to voice chords in a bebop style—top note of voicings no higher than G above middle C; don't double at the octave; roots are optional, since the bassist is playing them. Bassists do not like having the piano double their notes all the time, except on shuffles and Latin and manufactured grooves.

- In general, pianists can add 9ths, 11ths, 13ths and alterations as good taste dictates. In general, if the symbol is F7, that implies a 9th and 13th and possibly +11. If we want altered tensions we normally notate that (F7-9, F7+9, F7+5, etc). Tensions are optional. The music will sound fine without them. *(continued)*

CJCA III: WRITING FOR SMALL GROUPS

Example 4-4 *Mary's A Grand Old Name* quartet score, page 1

MARY – QUARTET ARRANGEMENT

Example 4-4 *Mary's A Grand Old Name* quartet score, page 2

CJCA III: WRITING FOR SMALL GROUPS

Example 4-4 *Mary's A Grand Old Name* quartet score, page 3

MARY – QUARTET ARRANGEMENT

Example 4-4 Mary's A Grand Old Name quartet score, page 4

CJCA III: WRITING FOR SMALL GROUPS

Example 4-4 Mary's A Grand Old Name quartet score, page 5

MARY – QUARTET ARRANGEMENT

Example 4-4 *Mary's A Grand Old Name* quartet score, page 6

- Less is more. The trumpet, bass and drums already sound good.
- Avoid clutter. Less is more.

Writing for Drums

If you need the drummer to play a groove (swing, samba, boogaloo, etc.), just write four slash marks (in 4/4 time) and the style of the groove (**A3-6**). He/she will know what to do. If there are specific rhythms that you require, write them in the stave with slashes and stems (**A1-2**). The word "Fill" means to improvise a figure to fill up those beats and set up the next band entrance. Make sure you tell the drummer if you want him to play sticks, brushes, mallets, hands, or whatever else you have in mind. This needs to be notated at the first measure of the chart. You can have him switch. He can play with one hand and two feet while he makes the switch.

[Let's listen to the head of **Mary** (letters **A** and **B**). We won't deal with the intro now, since I wrote it much later on. Is the melody clear? Can we still hear what Cohan had in mind? Is there a fresh point of view? Is there a nice balance of groove and interruption? When we get to the end of letter **B**, do we feel the need to launch into an improvised solo?]

Solos

After playing the melody chorus, it is traditional for players to solo. See letters **C** through **D** (see *Score* pp. 4-5/pp. 39-40). We can decide which players will solo and in what order. We can also predetermine how many choruses each player will get. In a quartet setting like this, it is traditional for the horn player and pianist to solo. Bass solos are less frequent, unless the leader is a bassist. Mike Richmond played bass with Horace Silver's quintet for 9 months and soloed only twice during the entire time... that's a bit extreme. Drum solos are generally reserved for up tempos, but there are exceptions.

Sometimes I leave the solo choices, order and length up to the leader or players. In cases like this, I might notate whom I need to go first or last.

Chord Changes

When providing chord changes for soloists and the accompanying rhythm section players, it is common (and generally advisable) to eliminate many or all of the fancy substitute changes and passing chords. Keep it simple. Players will either stick to the written changes or improvise their own tensions, passing chords and substitute changes.

Keep it Simple

There is a famous story about Roger Kellaway's first night playing with the Al Cohn/Zoot Sims Quintet at the Half Note. After the first set, Roger sat down with his wife in a booth. On the way back to the bandstand, Zoot walked by and leaned over to Roger, saying, "No altered chords."

Mickey Mouse

When the New Orleans clarinetist, Barney Bigard, joined Duke Ellington's band in 1928, he was baffled by Duke's harmonies. One of the horn players sitting next to him told him to ignore Ellington's voicings and just play on the basic changes. For the most part, this has been my philosophy. Making every chromatic change sounds Mickey Mouse.

If you are unfamiliar with the term "Mickey Mouse," it comes from film scoring. In animated cartoons, it is common to catch every bit of action in the score. If Mickey falls down, hit the tympani, etc. This can become obvious and predictable. In scoring films with live actors, we are careful not to overdo this sort of thing. When we overdo it, this over-stylization is called Mickey Mouse. I feel the same way about jazz players and writers who create lines that run an obstacle course through the chord changes.

Melody Comes First

When I first studied classical composition with Ludmila Ulehla, she would tell me that I was hearing the harmony and then writing the melody to fit my harmonies. She encouraged me to conceive of the melody first, and then let the melody determine the harmonies. I learned to free myself from predictable harmonies and melodies and became a much better melodist.

However, in arranging jazz music, we usually start with someone else's tune—their melody and harmonies. This limits us, but depending on the situation, we can exert varying degrees of freedom within these boundaries. When I am to solo, or write a new melody over a set of changes, I think of the basic harmonies, and where I am going. This may create some interesting dissonances with passing chords and substitute changes, but upon the resolution, all is forgiven. The listener is thinking, "Ooh, what's that... Ahh, I get it!" Tension and release. But if the melody has to follow the contours of the chord substitutions—the player may successfully complete the obstacle course, but the music will lose continuity and melodic integrity.

Play My Song

Something else for soloists and rhythm section compers to consider: It is their job to complete the arrangement. Monk used to tell tenor players, "Play my song." When Jimmy Hamilton joined Ellington's band, he asked Duke to write him the chord changes for his solos. Duke told him, "If I did that, you'd play all that s— that you practice. I want you to listen and play my song."

Wynton Marsalis tells professional musicians and student musicians, "Your first responsibility in a band is to learn the arrangements." Whatever you play, whether it's a written part, an improvised solo or improvised comping, it must relate to the arrangement. If you just play your favorite licks, rather than developing the ideas in the arrangement, the structure of the piece is weakened, and the overall music becomes superficial. Dizzy Gillespie used to talk about telling a story when you solo. The soloist's story must help to complete the arrangement's story.

Comping

It is generally left to the rhythm section to create its own accompaniment to solos. However, there are times when a written figure (which can be repeated) will be used as a send-off or as call-and-response. This sort of thing and the addition of written background figures becomes more common when we add more horns to our orchestration. We will deal with that in a later chapter.

Introduction

I have purposely left the introduction for last. When I wrote this chart, I didn't know what the intro would be. I just started writing at letter **A**. I figured that at some point, I'd write something that would *tell* me what the intro should be. This is pretty common for me. I rarely know the intro before I write the head. In fact many of my charts were completely written before I wrote the intro, so this is not unusual at all.

For me, writing intros is the hardest thing to do. A good intro should, in a few bars, predict what is going to happen in the piece, without giving away the surprises. Think of the greatest intro in all of jazz—*Take The "A" Train*. Duke's piano part encapsulates the entire chart in two measures. Intros don't get any better than that.

Introducing All Three Motifs

The pickup to the first measure is our 3-note chromatic motif transposed up a 4th. Then we have three repeated D's. That motif is then transposed up a 4th and up a 2nd. Rather than three B's, I used a chromatic lower neighbor (I love that chromatic motif) before finishing up with our old friend the dominant pedal D. Notice that the pentatonic motif is hinted at starting on the downbeat of the first bar: E, A, B, D. Add to all this the descending chromatic bass line. The written out piano part mimics the trumpet. The change in orchestration clears the way for a fresh trumpet statement of the melody.

[Let's listen to the entire arrangement now. This chart was meant to be charming. Nothing more, really. Does it succeed? Do you feel satisfied at the end? Remember that no arrangement can express everything you know or feel. Each piece conveys a small part of who you are. The goal is to be authentic and sincere. Music that tries to impress feels cheap—keep it real. We want people to relate to it, tap their foot, and be delighted.]

5. Mary's A Grand Old Name
Quintet Arrangement (2 Horns)

Rather than write and dissect a wholly new 2-horn arrangement, let's use the format of our 1-horn arrangement of **Mary**, and add a tenor saxophone part. Although I don't normally add a second horn part after an entire 1-horn arrangement is written, I mostly do conceive of the trumpet and bass part before adding the second horn (in this case, the tenor saxophone). Coincidentally, as I write this I am in the process of adding a trumpet part to a 1-horn chart for tenor sax and rhythm section, so this sort of thing does come up, and it's advantageous to know how to add creative and satisfying additional parts to pre-existing scores.

Before we begin, please understand that I chose trumpet and tenor sax since it is and has been the most common jazz quintet instrumentation since the 1950s. Assuming that I keep the trumpet as the top voice, I could have used alto sax, baritone sax or trombone for the second voice. All of those also have their precedents. In fact, the trumpet doesn't necessarily need to be the lead voice. We could choose any instrument.

When choosing a second horn, I usually opt for an instrument that contrasts in color and range with the lead instrument; e.g. brass/sax, trumpet/baritone sax. However, sometimes it's fun to use like instruments (Al Cohn/Zoot Sims Quintet—two tenors, Jay and Kai—two trombones) or two unlike instruments with similar ranges (Charlie Parker/Dizzy Gillespie Quintet—alto sax and trumpet, Gerry Mulligan Quartet with Bob Brookmeyer—baritone sax/valve trombone). Also consider less commonly used jazz instruments (flute, violin, bass clarinet, etc.)

I encourage you to listen to a wide variety of combinations of instruments. This is your palette. As we increase the size of the ensemble, we will make color decisions. The balance between homogeneous and heterogeneous colors is always a consideration. Some big band and orchestral arrangers only write for homogeneous sections. This is like in baseball when a pitcher only throws fastballs. He may be able to overpower some hitters, but he's not going to fool many of them. If he can mix in a few sliders, he's got more of a chance, and if he has a third pitch, like a change-up or curve, then he has the possibility of being a starting pitcher and going more than 6 innings. In orchestrating, as in baseball, a varied arsenal is essential for the long haul.

That said, let's go with adding a tenor sax. In the course of this arrangement of **Mary**, I use only a few textures (see *Score* and pp. 50-57). This gives the piece continuity. However, the ways that the textures are used vary, and hopefully will create the surprise necessary to counteract the continuity. The relationship of sameness and difference is crucial to all art and is always a major consideration.

Introduction

One texture available to us is to have one or the other horn play solo. Bear in mind that the difference between a solo and two or more instruments playing in unison is that solos have personality—they represent the individual (you, me, each one of us) in society. Unisons have no individual personality, and represent a group of people in agreement.

The opening pickup remains a solo for the trumpet (see **Score** p.1/pg. 50). He is joined by the tenor on the downbeat of the first measure. Instead of having the tenor play the same rhythms as the trumpet, I assigned him the rhythms played by the rhythm section. Each note gets its own chord. In most cases, the tenor part is voiced below the trumpet. This makes it clear to the listener which instrument is playing the melody.

There are three major considerations for which pitches to give the tenor. All three criteria must be met:

1. Intervallic relationship to the trumpet melody.
2. Relationship to the bass and piano harmonies.
3. Creation of a good melody for the tenor.

Most 2-part writing has been and continues to be in 3rds or 6ths.

Example 5-1

These consonant intervals always sound agreeable. No one ever questions them, but used too often, they can become too sweet. I like to employ a variety of intervals. No interval is out of bounds. It's all about context. Each interval elicits a different emotion from the listener. If I only used 3rds, it would confine my story to a narrow emotional range. The same goes for the exclusive use of any interval; 4ths, 7ths, etc. By changing the intervallic relationship between the trumpet and tenor, we create tension and release, which is the inner story of interesting music. Music that is devoid of tension and release quickly becomes predictable and boring.

Let's look at the intervals created between the trumpet and tenor: major 2nd, minor 6th, major 7th, and major 9th. Interesting, right? Their levels of dissonance/consonance are: mild dissonance, consonance, harsh dissonance, and soft dissonance. Tension and release. Also notice the contrary motion and finally oblique motion. I purposely chose this texture to oppose the constantly ascending trumpet melody. I like opposition in music as I do in the rest of life—it is challenging, and pushes us to greater depth and self-exploration and criticism, resulting in growth.

[Play the trumpet and tenor parts together. They oppose each other rhythmically, harmonically, and texturally. There is a lot of fight here.

Now let's see how the tenor and bass line up. They are in rhythmic unison with consonant intervals: major 10th, minor 10th, minor 10th, and major 10th—all his notes are the 3rd of each chord. They move in parallel descending motion, with the exception of the final note, which is in oblique motion. The disagreeableness of the trumpet and tenor is counteracted by the unquestioned agreement between the tenor and bass. The harmonies in the piano fill out the other notes in the chords. If we didn't have a piano (or other chordal instrument), the music would work just fine, because of the strength of the intervallic relationships, their opposite natures and textures, and the tension and release.]

Thirds and Sevenths

You've probably noticed that, unlike the tenor part, which is almost exclusively thirds and sevenths, the trumpet melody contains almost no thirds and sevenths. For the most part, thirds and sevenths are inside parts. The other notes make more interesting melody notes and are easier to harmonize. We will deal with this later.

Good Melody Writing

There is one more important element at work here: good melody writing. By that, I don't just mean the trumpet melody, but all the melodies; the trumpet, the bass, and the tenor. Add to that also the piano notes. The **voice leading** of each note in each chord to the next notes in the next chord.

Voice leading is a term that is mostly misunderstood. When harmony is taught in books, lessons and schools, students are usually told that good voice leading (the melodies made up of the other voices of the chord below the melody) consists of repeated notes or stepwise motion (**parsimonious** voice leading). Although this formula may work in many cases, it is an oversimplification, and fails to see the big picture.

Good voice leading means writing good melodies for each instrument or voice. Those melodies should be singable, and should sound good when played or sung in conjunction with every other part. This is crucial in choral/vocal writing, since singers must hear their pitches. They don't have buttons or keys to press down like instrumentalists have. If we carry this same principle over to instrumental writing, each player, having a good melody, will approach his part with authenticity and purpose. Playing parts with melodically unsatisfying shapes becomes an intellectual exercise and lessens the impact and integrity of the music.

In general we tend to limit the interval skips in the inner parts to less than the intervals in the melody. Larger skips tend to draw our attention. Of course, if we want to draw our attention to an inner part or parts, larger intervals work beautifully. It is common for bass parts to jump around. 4ths and 5ths generally abound, but other intervals are possible as well as long as the bass has a convincing melody. Sometimes we like to use inversions or diminished chords to smooth things out into stepwise bass movement.

Look at the bass part for the Intro. It starts out with descending chromatics using a passing diminished (B♭°) and a tritone sub (A♭7-5 rather than D7). When the piano answers, the bass starts with the same Bm11, but then uses B♭7-5 rather than B♭°. This allows the B♭ chord to resolve down a perfect 5th to E♭9-5 and then down another perfect 5th to A♭7+5+11. Note the contrary motion between the bass and the top notes in the piano.

Independence of Parts

When creating a second part (in this case the tenor part), I make sure that I avoid both the melody notes (trumpet part) and bass notes (bass part). This assures us of three independent parts. An easy way to create the tenor part is to give him either the 3rd or the 7th of each chord, making sure that the note you choose is not in the trumpet or bass. This is a bit formulaic, but it can sound interesting if the melody creates interesting intervals with the second part, which is the case in our intro. Later on in the chart, we will explore other options.

Complete Chords

Since we only have 2 horns and a bassist, the greatest amount of pitches we can have in a chord is three (the piano notes don't count). Since most jazz chords involve four different pitches (4-part harmony), we can't possibly write complete chords, so there is no need to try. There are going to be missing chord tones. The sonorities will sound good if the intervallic relationships between the parts are strong, the individual melodies are strong and there is a satisfying design of tension and release.

The Head

The overall texture for the melody chorus (the head) is trumpet melody with the tenor joining the rhythm section's accompaniment. This was set up in the Intro. There are a few key spots where the trumpet and tenor are in rhythmic unison, but never do they play the same pitches.

MARY – QUINTET ARRANGEMENT

Unisons

Be aware that this textural scheme is not common in jazz. The great majority of 2-horn writing either has the horns in unison or in octave unison. If and when relief is needed, they might move into harmony. The choice between unison and octaves depends on the best range for the instruments. For instance, if the trumpet plays in his upper register, unison would be above the tenor's range. Conversely, if the trumpet is in his lower register, that could be below the tenor's ideal range. Write parts that sound good and are fun to play. I like to challenge players a bit, but not so much that they have poor control or a low percentage of accuracy.

Choosing Textures and Harmonies

My choice of textures and harmonies for this tune had a lot to do with the diatonic nature of the melody and the medium tempo. Had the melody been more angular and chromatic, that would have provided sufficient interest for a unison treatment. Also, faster tempi demand unison for 8th note passages in small group writing. As we add more horns, we tend to harmonize more. Here, I suggest you listen to Horace Silver's recordings. Up-tempo *Room 608* is played in unison, while the medium tempo *The Preacher* is in 2-part harmony.

More Thirds and Sevenths

Bars **A1-6** follow the same procedure of hooking the tenor up with the piano and bass rhythms, and giving him either the 3rd or 7th of each chord. Many of these rhythms coincide with the trumpet rhythms. There is a certain amount of agreement and disagreement in each measure, until we get to measure **A7** where the trumpet is clearly in a call-and-response with the others, and the tenor plays more dissonant notes (the 9th of the E♭7 chord and the +5 of the A♭7). The next measure is also call-and-response, but the tenor reverts to playing the consonant 7ths of the chords.

Repetition: Emphasizing the Form

When the melody from letter **A** returns, I use the exact same orchestration for **B1-3** as I did in **A1-3**. This makes it easier for the listener to understand the form of the piece. It also makes it easier on the players by not challenging them with new material to learn. My philosophy is to repeat material when possible, but not to the point of becoming predictable. Repetition gives a piece character.

More of the Same, Only More So

The last 4 bars of the head proceed with the same techniques for the tenor part as before. Every note in that part is either a 3rd or 7th of the chord with the exception of the second beat of **B5**, which is the +5. That is an interesting spot. The trumpet is ascending basically chromatically, and has the 3rd of the chord on beat two. If we followed the descending tenor part in that bar, we would have E, E♭, D. The E♭

CJCA III: WRITING FOR SMALL GROUPS

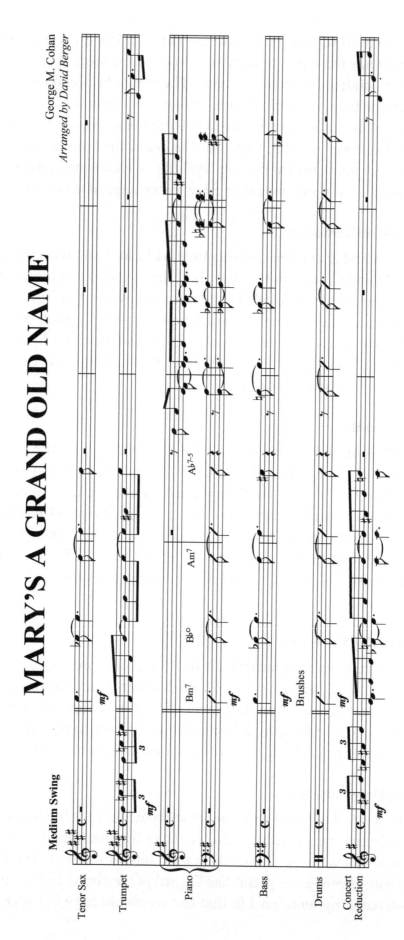

Example 5-2 *Mary's A Grand Old Name* quintet score, page 1

Example 5-2 Mary's A Grand Old Name quintet score, page 2

CJCA III: WRITING FOR SMALL GROUPS

Example 5-2 *Mary's A Grand Old Name* quintet score, page 3

MARY – QUINTET ARRANGEMENT

Mary's A Grand Old Name

	Solos															
Ten	A	G⁷	C#m⁷	F#⁷	Bm⁷	E⁷	A	D⁷	C#m⁷	C°	E	Am⁶	Abm⁷ G°	F#m⁷	Bm⁷	E⁷
Tpt	A	G⁷	C#m⁷	F#⁷	Bm⁷	E⁷	A	D⁷	C#m⁷	C°	E	Am⁶	Abm⁷ G°	F#m⁷	Bm⁷	E⁷
Piano	G	F⁷	Bm⁷	E⁷	Am⁷	D⁷	G	C⁷	Bm⁷	B♭°	D/A	Gm⁶	F#m⁷ F°	Em⁷	Am⁷	D⁷
Bass	G	F⁷	Bm⁷	E⁷	Am⁷	D⁷	G	C⁷	Bm⁷	B♭°	D/A	Gm⁶	F#m⁷ F°	Em⁷	Am⁷	D⁷
Drums				⁄.									⁄.			
Reduction	G	F⁷	Bm⁷	E⁷	Am⁷	D⁷	G	C⁷	Bm⁷	B♭°	D/A	Gm⁶	Gbm⁷ F°	Em⁷	Am⁷	D⁷

© 2015 Such Sweet Thunder, Inc.
All Rights Reserved

Example 5-2 Mary's A Grand Old Name quintet score, page 4

CJCA III: WRITING FOR SMALL GROUPS

Example 5-2 Mary's A Grand Old Name quintet score, page 5

MARY – QUINTET ARRANGEMENT

Example 5-2 *Mary's A Grand Old Name* quintet score, page 6

CJCA III: WRITING FOR SMALL GROUPS

Example 5-2 *Mary's A Grand Old Name* quintet score, page 7

Example 5-2 *Mary's A Grand Old Name* quintet score, page 8

is enharmonically equivalent to D# (the 3rd of B7), and would be an octave unison with the trumpet. This could be acceptable, since they are in contrary motion, but I prefer using the G (the +5) instead. It adds interest harmonically and melodically.

Catching the Syncopations

You've probably noticed that most of the syncopations in the trumpet part are caught in the tenor and rhythm section. This comes to a head in **B6** where the first four notes are in rhythmic unison, and notes two, three, and four are syncopations. For me, this is a fun moment to play and hear. We haven't had that many syncopations in a row, nor have we had everyone agree on four successive notes.

Solos

It's rare to use horn backgrounds in 2-horn charts, so we will just let the rhythm section accompany the soloists (see *Score* p. 6/p. 55) as we did in the quartet version of **Mary**. The reasoning here is that, if one horn plays a background for another horn, it could be confusing to the listener. To put it into football terms: who is carrying the ball, and who is a blocker? Backgrounds for piano solos are rare because the horns will by their very nature dominate and make the piano sound weak. However, I often write very soft backgrounds behind bass solos. Alternatives to backgrounds are send-offs (ensemble figures at the top of the form that lead into a solo) and call-and-response figures.

Shout Chorus

Following the solos, it is normal in a small group setting to play the head again (Recapitulation). Sometimes we feel ambitious and want to develop our ideas more before returning to the melody. In the great majority of cases, we write a new melody over a chorus of the chord changes to our tune. This is called the shout chorus or sock chorus. Aside from telling more of the story, it builds to the climax of the arrangement (the *and*-of-beat-2 in **E6**—see *Score* p. 6/p. 55). Because the climax comes less than half way through the shout, a secondary climax occurs at **F5** (see *Score* p. 7/p. 56).

Changing the Groove

The most noticeable thing about this shout chorus is the shift from 4/4 back to 2-beat. The head was in 2, the solos in 4; and now shifting back to 2 gives us a relaxed feeling that is reminiscent of the head. Most shout choruses don't switch gears, but there are some notable famous examples like Frank Foster's *Shiny Stockings*, written for Count Basie. In that chart, Frank wrote two shout choruses. The first was soft and in 2. He then switches to 4/4 for the loud shout chorus. If you don't know this chart, you need to! Shifting from 2 to 4 and vice versa feels like shifting gears in a car. When you go from 4/4 to 2, it feels slower, but it's not, and conversely, shifting from 2 to 4 feels like it's faster, but again, it's not. This is a subtle and most useful option.

Stay Close to the Motifs

In developing my trumpet line in **E** and **F**, I used three ideas.

1. The opening descending pentatonic motif (**A1-2**). This diatonic pattern consists of descending minor 3rd, major 2nd, perfect 4th.
2. Ascending chromatic motif that appears at **A7** and in diminution at **B5**.
3. The repeated dominants (D) in **A6**.

Limiting myself to these three ideas gives this chorus unity and impact. The fewer the ideas, the more I can develop each one. If I had twelve ideas, there would be no time to develop them; I could only state each one and move on. This would make the music superficial.

Depth of expression is attained through development of the fewest number of ideas. The more opposite those ideas are, the broader the scope of the music. These are two elements of great art. A third element is universality: Does this music describe our culture (In my case, how it feels to be an American), and beyond that, a human being?

Pentatonic Motif

Let's take out our musical microscopes and zero in on the details of the shout chorus. The first four trumpet notes at **E** are the first four melody notes of the tune (our descending pentatonic). I disguised it by changing the rhythm. There is a nice balance of tensions and chord tones: D is the 5th of G, B is the +11 of F7, resolving to A, the 3rd of the chord, and finally, E, which is the 11th of Bm7.

Chromatic Motif

The next eight beats repeat the ascending chromatic *sol, si, la* motif over moving chord changes. Each time the figure repeats it sounds different, because the underlying harmonies are different. This sensation of staying the same while everything else changes is akin to our existence on this planet. I am sitting still in my chair while the earth turns on its axis. This is the principle behind pedal point.

Back to the Pentatonic Motif

The second half of **E4** through the first half of **E6** is all based on our pentatonic motif. Instead of descending, we play the first three notes of the motif in retrograde before changing direction and reversing the order (3, 2, 1, 2, 3). The fourth note (E) appears next, and then we repeat the B and A before leaping up to an F#.

Where did that come from? In the original 4-note motif, the last interval is a descending perfect 4th (A down to E). We have already jumped up to the E.

We went A up to E in **E5**—an ascending perfect 5th. This is a slight expansion of the perfect 4th interval. We are gradually widening the intervals. So, in the next measure we jump up from A to F# (a major 6th)—again expanding slightly. This expansion is very clear. We all hear it. Our process sounds logical, so we accept it. Reaching up to the F# is the climax of the chart. It's the highest note for the trumpet as well as being the biggest jump (widest interval).

Now, Back to the Chromatic Motif

We seem to be alternating between these two ideas. **E7** is the chromatic motif starting on A instead of D and repeated three times. I preceded it with a G#, which is the chromatic lower neighbor to the A (extending our 3-note chromatic pattern to four notes) and relating to the previous F#. It's a step higher, but displaced down an octave. Actually, this drop of a minor 7th is the widest interval in the shout chorus, adding to the climactic effect in **E6**.

Returning to the Scene of the Crime

In **E8**, we return to F#, but this time it is an octave lower than it was in **E6**. To give it some juice, I made it the +9 of an Eb7 chord and then slid down a half-step to F natural, which is the +9 of D7. Sliding down that half-step is a 2-note inversion of our chromatic motif. Sneaky how the subconscious does all this stuff!

Time for Something New

To signal the new 8-bar section (letter **F**—see *Score* p. 7/p. 56), we need a fresh idea. This is where the repeated dominant pedals come in. In the head, we alternated those pedals with other pitches, but here I'm mostly repeating the pedal notes in a stutter effect. We start with a 3-note pickup that leads to a B on the downbeat— an ascending major 6th, which sounds friendly, since we just heard it in **E6**. It's reassuring when things come back, and it's subtle when they come back in different places in the phrase, or on different beats in the bar. I like this B-and-three E's figure, so I'll repeat it twice before going back to the original repeated E's (twelve of them).

Mixing It All Up Together

As in the *stretto* section of a fugue, we can create the illusion of everything moving faster while keeping the same tempo. Just like a *stretto*, where the space between the entrances of the themes is condensed, we can use all three of our motifs close together, and integrate them.

F4 begins on the twelfth repetition of our old friend D, which then becomes the first note of our 3-note chromatic motif. Instead of following the motif with an eighth rest, so that the repetition will begin on the same part of the beat, the repetition of the figure begins an eighth-note early, suggesting a 3/8 measure (like the motif of *In The Mood* and the clarinet solo in Jelly Roll Morton's *Black Bottom*

Stomp). This is followed by ascending and descending perfect 5ths (E, B, E). The E's are repeated a total of three times (this refers to our repeated D's, only up a step). Then it's back to our 3-note chromatic motif, only this time it is preceded by a chromatic lower neighbor, producing a 4-note version.

This is followed by another 3-note chromatic motif, but transposed up a half-step. Then it's back down to the original chromatic motif (starting on D), but this time we start on D for a quarter note, go to the final E of the motif, jump up a perfect 5th to B, and then complete the motif in retrograde (backwards): E♭, D. This final 5-note phrase is the intellectual climax of the chart. I say that because it subtly melds the three motifs together: repeated D's, the upward perfect 5th jump suggesting the pentatonic motif, and the inversion (also retrograde) of the chromatic motif. If that wasn't enough, this figure ending on D smoothly leads us to the pick-up to the recapitulation, which also starts on D. (I love that repeated D motif).

Melody-Bass Relationship

[Now go back to letter **E** and play the trumpet and bass parts together. Notice how they have an interesting relationship. Sometimes they are consonant, and sometimes they are dissonant. You never really know which will come next, but when it does, it feels perfectly natural. Although there are quite a few tensions in the trumpet part, it never feels weird.]

Melody-Harmony Relationships

[Next, slowly play the harmonies below the trumpet part. Notice how I pretty much kept the harmonies that we used for soloing, but added a few passing chords and substitutions to give the trumpet notes better tension and release, and to avoid unnecessary unisons between the bass and trumpet. For instance, in **E2**, since the trumpet has an E concert, I don't want to use an E7 on the 3rd beat. The B♭7 (tritone substitute) gives us more independence of parts.

Another such situation is at **F1**. Rather than move directly from G to F7, since there are all those repeated D's in the trumpet, I inserted the F#m7 to delay the resolution to F7, which creates more suspense. Also notice all the chromatic bass notes. They are nearly all descending, which is in contrary motion to the chromatic motif in the trumpet part. I love when the foreground and background are so integrated. I didn't plan this... in fact, I didn't even notice it, until writing this chapter. The music just wanted to go that way.]

Adding the Tenor Sax Part

At letter **E**, as we relax back into the easy 2-beat reminiscent of the head, we also use a similar texture to the one we did back then. The trumpet alternates between being independent and in concert with the tenor. During the head, the tenor hooks up with the rhythm section rhythmically. For the shout, the rhythm section just plays a basic 2-beat until the very last bar (**F8**), where the tenor and rhythm section are concerted, leading to a short break that sets up the pickup back to the head. Breaks are a highly effective tool for defining the form.

Catching Syncopations

The tenor starts letter **E** (see *Score* p. 6/p. 55) catching the syncopations in the trumpet part with 3rds and 7ths. This goes on for four bars until **E5**, where the horns play four bars of rhythmic unison, except for **E7**, where the tenor holds out a whole note while the trumpet plays repeated 8th note triplets. Mixed in with the usual 3rds and 7ths in the tenor are:

- A diminished 7th on the B♭°.
- A major 6th on the Gm6.
- A diminished 5th on the F°.

All these notes make for smooth melodies for the tenor and pleasing sonorities with the trumpet while breaking up the predictability of 3rds and 7ths. I should point out that I normally don't rely on 3rds and 7ths so much. It varies from chart to chart. This particular situation seemed to call for this more conservative approach. Once these sonorities were established, I continued to run with them and only deviated for a temporary effect.

For the most part, letter **F** (see *Score* p. 7/p. 56) is confined to 3rds and 7ths. The primary interest continues to be the rhythmic independence and confluence of the trumpet and tenor. The tenor notes add emphasis and harmonic interest to the trumpet melody. The deviations from our formula grab our ear.

The downbeat of **F2** has the tenor on the ♭5 of the Bm7-5 chord. This is an interesting spot. Normally we would expect a Bm7 (with a perfect 5th —F#). The F natural is a blue note (♭7th in the key of G) and gives us a temporary blues feeling. It's just slight, but much appreciated. In half diminished chords (m7-5), the most important note is the ♭5 for two reasons: It is the only note that distinguishes it from the diatonic m7 chord, and the ♭5 creates a tritone interval with the bass note (in this case F and B). Also note that the F♮ gives the tenor line an interesting shape.

On the third and fourth beats of that same measure (**F2**), the trumpet has repeated Ds, which are the 3rd of the B♭7 chord. Rather than give the tenor the 7th below that, I have him repeat Cs (the 9th of the chord), which then remain common tones in the next measure (as the 3rds of both the Am7 and A♭7). The use of the 9th and the major 2nd interval it creates with the trumpet are both justified when the chord changes to Am7. This is a classic *appoggiatura*. We don't need to justify most tensions in jazz, but it is reassuring when we do.

Measure **F4** is an anomaly, in that it contains the only trumpet/tenor unisons in the entire chart. Because of that, our ear is drawn to it. I suppose I chose to highlight this spot because of the interesting 3/8 use of the chromatic motif. Had I just given the tenor a B dotted half note (the 3rd of the G chord) and then a B♭ quarter note (the 7th of the C7), it would have sounded okay, but we probably would not have taken notice of the implied 3/8 bars. Honestly, I wasn't consciously thinking about this (or much else when I wrote the tenor part), but it felt satisfying to have the trumpet and tenor agree for this figure.

The next note (the *and*-of-4 in **F4** tied over into the next measure) reintroduces the Bm7. Since we had a Bm7-5 a few measures earlier, it feels fresh to have the tenor play the F# (the natural 5th of the chord) rather than the 3rd or 7th. The rest of letter **F** is all 3rds and 7ths.

[Listen to the shout chorus (letters **E** and **F**). Play the trumpet part by itself on the piano. Is it a compelling melody? Now play the trumpet and bass together. Hear how they relate in a consonant way. This makes possible the dissonance in the trumpet part.

Now, play the tenor part by itself on the piano. Is it a compelling melody? Then, play the tenor and bass together. Hear how they relate in a consonant way. This makes possible the dissonance in the trumpet part.

Next, play the tenor and trumpet parts alone, paying attention to the tension and release. Finally, listen to all the parts together. It doesn't sound as dissonant as you might think, right?

About 40 years ago, I was playing a rehearsal with the Gerry Mulligan Concert Jazz Band. After playing *Bweebida Bobbida*, which was arranged by Bob Brookmeyer, I told Bob that I was surprised at how much dissonance there was in the arrangement. I had listened to the recording for many years, and it sounded pretty consonant—interesting, but consonant. But when playing my part, I was constantly rubbing against other parts. An almost imperceptible smile crept across Bob's face, so I knew something witty and pithy was on its way. He said that he had learned how to sneak dissonance into his music from all his years of writing commercial music. This lesson was not lost on me. In fact, it has much to do with my approach here. Thanks, Bob.]

Recap and Coda

After the shout chorus, we return to the first 12 bars of the head (**A1-B4**) before going to the coda. All the tenor notes in the coda are either 3rds or 7ths except for the second beat of the first bar of the coda (the +5 on the B9+5 chord) and two bars later the ♭5 on the D♭7-5. All the concerted voicings (trumpet, tenor and rhythm section in rhythmic unison) give the coda weight and finality. Reverting to the final two bars of the head in the final two bars of the chart tie up the package with a recognizable and comfortable ribbon and bow.

[Give the entire chart a listen and see if it holds together. I wasn't trying to do anything earth-shattering in this piece. All I was looking for was something nice and comfortable, but that would still make you think just a bit.]

6. Mary, Getting Grander
Sextet Arrangement (3 Horns)

While Horace Silver was my main influence for quintet writing, Benny Golson's writing for his Jazztet taught me how to get the most mileage out of three horns. Their instrumentation was trumpet, tenor saxophone, trombone, piano, bass, and drums. If we just add a trombone to our quintet version of **Mary**, we can convert it into a sextet chart.

The Trombone
Although the trombone reads in concert pitch in the bass clef, it is really a B♭ instrument pitched an octave below the trumpet. When the trumpet and trombone play in octaves, they are perfectly balanced.

Awkward Slide Movement
Problems can occur when the trumpet dips down into the low register. Writing the bone an octave lower can present some awkward slide positions. Moving from first to seventh position and vice versa is awkward. It's possible in some cases, but be very careful. To avoid slide problems, it is always safe to write the trombone from E in the middle of the bass clef up to C (an octave above middle C). The octave below that is useful, but should be avoided in fast moving passages that involve big slide movements (more than 2 positions). Above the middle E, there are alternate slide positions that can be used to keep the movement smooth. Unless you are writing for beginners, I wouldn't worry too much about any of this. You'd be surprised how clever and adept trombonists are.

Higher Pitched vs. Lower Pitched Instruments
One of my favorite sextet recordings when I was a teenager was the J.J. Johnson record of *Get Happy*. The three horns were J.J. on trombone, Jimmy Heath on tenor sax, and Clifford Brown on trumpet. When I was in grad school, I transcribed all three solos and wrote a paper about them. Each soloist played two choruses. One thing I discovered was that J.J. played 216 notes, Jimmy played 300-plus notes and Clifford Brown played over 500 notes.

Since then I have transcribed thousands of solos. What I have found is that the higher pitched the instrument (trumpet, flute, alto sax, etc.)—the more notes, and the lower pitched (trombone, baritone sax, bass, etc.)—the fewer. This has to do with the ability of those instruments in some cases, and more importantly with the overtone series and how we hear music. Think about the piccolo and clarinet parts in Sousa marches. Now think about the trombone and tuba parts. Although

CJCA III: Writing for Small Groups

trombonists, bari sax players, and bassists have worked hard to be able to play fast, this goes against their basic function in the music and the listener's need for a solid bottom. Although I strive to write interesting melodies for the lower instruments, I generally don't overburden them with fast moving 8th note and 16th note lines.

Back in the 1940s, Louis Armstrong was asked what he thought about bebop. His answer was that everyone was playing the clarinet part. How perceptive—but of course, I would think no less of Louis Armstrong.

Voicing the Trombone and Tenor

Since the tenor sax and the trombone have similar ranges,

Example 6-1 Trombone range.

they naturally sound good in unison. When writing horns in harmony or in counterpoint, where one part is higher than the other, we must decide which instrument gets the upper note. This was easy with trumpet and tenor, since the trumpet is much brighter and has a much higher range.

Depending on the abilities and sounds of the players, we can write some passages with the trombone above the tenor and some with him below. My general procedure is to write the trombone above the tenor except when the part goes high (above F in the treble clef) or when it goes below the tenor's range. Many tenor players are not adept at playing subtone, so I would avoid writing low notes for them. Let's take a look at the trombone part for **Mary** (see *Score* and pp. 70-77).

Introduction

While the tenor plays descending 3rds of the chords, I gave the bone the descending 7ths. Combined with the roots in the bass, this gives us an almost full chord sound. The root gives us the context for the chord and the 3rd and 7th give us the color. The trumpet notes add interest. This is very safe and ordinary. It makes us feel secure.

Write What Sounds Good to You

As I've said before, my note choices came from my sense of what sounds good to me. All the structural explanations I'm about to tell you may have been deep in my brain somewhere, and they make sense, but I was not really aware of most of them at the time of writing. It's good to know all this and feed it into your subconscious, but if you make your musical decisions based solely on the theory, your music will be too linear at best, and mechanical and sterile at worst. Learn how music functions, and then follow your instinct. Save the analysis for afterwards, at which point, you should be most critical; and be ready to make adjustments where needed.

The Head

(See *Score* pp. 2-3/pp. 71-72.) Although there are a lot of 3rds and 7ths in the tenor and trombone parts during the head, things get more complicated, especially when the trumpet plays either of those notes, and the tenor or trombone avoids them. In most cases, the trombone plays either the 3rd or 7th of the chord with occasional roots or 5ths. The lower the part, generally, the more functional. The exception to this is for linear purposes (to create a good melodic line for the bone).

Adding Roots and 5ths in the Trombone

At **A1** the trombone plays the 3rds of the chords while the tenor has the 7ths and the trumpet moves from the 13th of F7 to the 5th of E7. With the bassist on the roots of these chords, we have a nice full sound. **A2** presents a different situation. The trumpet starts with the 7th of the Bm7. The tenor supplies the 3rd; rather than having the trombone play the 5th (F#), I opted for him to play the root (B). My reasoning was that the F# created a D major triad with the tenor and trumpet A and D. This sounded too bright for my taste. Giving the trombone the root on the bottom (in unison with the bass) creates a more complex sound, which I think suits the mood better.

On the next chord, the trumpet plays E (the enharmonic ♭5 of the B♭7), which allows the tenor and trombone to revert to their 3rd and 7th routine. Similarly in the next measure (**A3**), we start with 3rds and 7ths, but then, on the fourth beat, the trumpet disrupts this pattern and plays the 7th of the A♭7 chord and the 6th of the G chord. The tenor has the 3rd of both chords, pushing the trombone down to the 5ths. With the bass playing the roots, we make this cadence in very satisfying, complete 4-part harmony.

Contrary Motion

There is a sweet little moment in the trombone in the next 5 bars (**A4-8**). Notice how the tenor moves parallel with the trumpet for the first three notes, but then is in contrary motion with him for the next three bars. What do we do with the trombone? The trombone starts parallel with the tenor for three notes, is contrary for the next three, and then is parallel for the rest of the phrase, thereby resulting in some contrary motion in the horns through every note. Also note the nice little diatonic sequence the bone plays: we have *la*, *ti*, *do* in **A4-5**, followed by the sequence a step lower (*sol*, *la*, *ti*) and then a return to the starting *la*. It's refreshing to have so much diatonicism in the midst of all this chromaticism.

Let's look at the harmonies that the bone is playing. In **A4** he has the 3rd of **C7**. There's nothing new here, but then he moves to the 5th of the Bm7, while the trumpet has the 7th and the tenor the 3rd. I didn't want this D major sonority three bars earlier because it would have sounded too bright and simplistic. Why does it work here? Contrary motion and the diatonic sequence.

Notice how we move from this D major triad (over the B in the bass) to a quartal voicing (the trumpet and tenor form a perfect 4th while the trombone is an augmented 4th below the tenor and a major 7th below the trumpet. This unstable voicing is a favorite of jazz pianists and arrangers everywhere. In this key, it's normally used over an A (A13) or an E♭ (E♭7+9). In this case there is a B♭ in the bass, which creates a B♭°. The F♯ is a tension (a whole step above the ♭5), which resolves to the ♭5 (E) on the next beat. Rather than repeat the B♭° voicing without the tension on top, I just let the trumpet play the E by himself. *Sometimes what you leave out is as important as what you put in.*

In **A6**, because of the inversion (D/A) and the interesting contrary motion, the trombone plays the root of the D chord before moving up in stepwise fashion to the 6th of Gm and the root of F♯m7, and then down to the root of Em7. It may seem strange to use all these roots, but on the inverted D chord, the bass has the 5th, so giving the bone the root helps to define the chord. As far as the roots on the minor 7th chords, I often prefer the sound of 1, 3, 7 or the plain minor triad 1, 3, 5 to 3, 5, 7 or 3, 7, 5—the latter two voicings containing the major triad built on the third of the minor chord. As I mentioned before, this often sounds too bright and simplistic for my taste.

A7 has the tenor joining the trumpet in upper structure notes (tensions). On the E♭9 the trumpet has the +11 and the tenor the 9th. This leaves both the 3rd and 7th available for the bone. I chose the 7th because it created a complex augmented triad with the other two horns.

On the A♭9+5, I just had the bone slide down a half-step to the 3rd, producing contrary motion with the trumpet, which is ascending chromatically. In the following bar the tenor and bone revert to 7ths and 3rds, while the trumpet holds out his B (which is the +11 of F7, the 5th of E7+9, and the +5 of E♭7-5). All this complicated stuff, and we are only halfway through the head!

Repeating bars **A1-3** in **B1-3** comes as a welcome relief—a chance for the listeners to catch their breath and digest what they have heard. As far as the trombone part is concerned, **B4-7** is all 7ths and 3rds.

The Leading Tone Amen

The final answer to the trumpet in **B8** is a leading tone amen (VII to I). Rather than dressing it up with tensions, I just use major triads, so that it is pure and recognizable to everyone. Since the trumpet has the root on top, the bass has the roots on the bottom, and the tenor has the 3rds, I gave the bone the missing 5ths.

[Let's listen to the chart up to this point. Do you hear how the bone adds harmonic depth without disturbing the message of the original quintet chart? While the quintet chart sounded just fine, the sextet is just a bit fuller and more interesting harmonically. I encourage you to play the trombone part by itself. How does it work melodically? Then play the bone and the bass together. This tells you how the bone functions harmonically. Next play the tenor and bone together, the bone and trumpet, and then all three horns. *Every part needs to relate well to every other part.* This is important in every chart you write, but *even more so the fewer instruments you have,* because each part is more exposed.]

Solos

Where in the quartet and quintet versions, we just let the soloists be accompanied by the rhythm section; now that we have three horns, it is possible to have two of them play a background for the third. In the case of this chart, I chose to write a background for the trumpet solo (see **Score** pp. 4-5/pp. 73-74), but I could just as easily have chosen a background for either the tenor or bone. I suppose I chose the trumpet because it is featured on the head. This chart is almost a trumpet feature.

Writing Backgrounds

The purpose of backgrounds is to create a setting that will not only make the soloist sound good, but also inspire him to rise to greatness. There are other very important things going on here:

A change of texture and orchestration. This relieves the monotony of piano, bass and drum accompaniment.

Motivic development. It is incumbent on the arranger to further the story presented in the intro and head.

Backgrounds keep the rhythm section and soloists in the story of this chart, contributing relevant material rather than merely playing stock licks.

Motivic Development vs. Leaving Room for the Soloist

As I write this next section, I pray that I have stuck to the motifs of this chart and moved them forward just a bit. I say "pray" because until now, I have not analyzed what I wrote. Hopefully, I will find that I have practiced what I preach. My thoughts while writing this background at **C** and **D** were to keep the character of the piece while leaving the trumpet enough space to be creative. I didn't want to push him into a corner. As you can see and hear, there are busy measures followed by more sparse writing. I leave it up to the soloist whether to rest during the busy spots or blow through them. The one thing that *doesn't* work is for the soloist and

CJCA III: WRITING FOR SMALL GROUPS

Example 6-2 *Mary's A Grand Old Name* sextet score, page 1

Example 6-2 *Mary's A Grand Old Name* sextet score, page 2

CJCA III: WRITING FOR SMALL GROUPS

Example 6-2 *Mary's A Grand Old Name* sextet score, page 3

Example 6-2 Mary's A Grand Old Name sextet score, page 4

CJCA III: WRITING FOR SMALL GROUPS

Example 6-2 *Mary's A Grand Old Name* sextet score, page 5

MARY – SEXTET ARRANGEMENT

Example 6-2 Mary's A Grand Old Name sextet score, page 6

CJCA III: WRITING FOR SMALL GROUPS

Example 6-2 *Mary's A Grand Old Name* sextet score, page 7

MARY – SEXTET ARRANGEMENT

Example 6-2 *Mary's A Grand Old Name* sextet score, page 8

the background to come to rest at the same moment. I expect the soloist to listen and respond appropriately.

Combining Motifs

In the course of development, it is quite common to combine motifs. We don't want to be too obvious in this endeavor. We want things to feel natural and organic. The first four and a half bars of **C** uses both our opening pentatonic motif and then morphs into our chromatic motif. With the exception of the C in **C2**, we have nearly four bars of the four notes in a G6 (E, D, G, B). To complete the G pentatonic scale, we need only the missing A, which occurs on the downbeat of **C5**. The drama of holding off the last note of the scale is heightened by a chromatic approach from above (B to B♭ to A)—the inversion of our 3-note chromatic motif. Now, what about that C in **C2**? Why, that's a chromatic pickup to our motif, much as we are going to do, going from **E5-6**.

Sequences and Expanding Intervals

Are you wondering about where the F# in **C5-6** came from? Go back two bars. We have an ascending perfect 5th interval. **C5-6** is a modified sequence of that—it's a perfect 4th higher and I've expanded the perfect 5th slightly to a major 6th. The impression of a sequence draws our attention and the inter-vallic expansion makes it feel heroic. We have reached higher and made it.

Ornamentation

The 16th note pickups in **C6** are simply stylistic ornamentation. They help keep the rhythms from becoming predictable while introducing a previously unheard blue note. Up until now the background line is all diatonic G major, with the exception of the blue note B♭ in **C4**. Blue notes, even when they are of short duration or hidden inside harmonies, give us a feeling of the blues. I like the blues. I hope you do, too. The blues feels sexy to me.

Chromatic Motif in Diminution with Addition and Subtraction

C7 has the chromatic motif in its original ascending form and key (D, D#, E). Instead of quarter notes (as in **B5**), we have sped it up to 8th notes (diminution). The B from the pickup to **C6** comes back twice in **C7** as added connectors—first to the lead to a truncated (shortened) 2-note version of the chromatic motif and then to the repeated note motif in **C8**. Note how the D# in the truncated version forms the +11 of the A7 chord. The trombone moves up chromatically to finish the phrase with repeated E's. We thought we were being cheated, and then, surprise, we get not only one E, but also 3 more E's in succession. In **C8** the trombone dips down to play 3 G's resolving to an F# (the 7th of Am7 to the 3rd of D7). Then the bone and tenor go back into unison to play the three tonic stuttering pickups to letter **D**.

MARY – SEXTET ARRANGEMENT

More Repeated Notes and 3rd/7th Resolution

D2-3 has the tenor and bone extending the repeated note motif by one note, while resolving the 7ths to 3rds. Rather than giving the tenor the 7th on the Am7, I had him resolve up to the B (the 9th of Am7). This is a bit shocking (it rubs against the C, which is a half-step higher in the bone). What makes it kosher is the melodic strength of how it got there (*do, ti, re* in the key of A minor).

More Blue Notes

We introduced a couple of short blue notes in letter **C** (B♭ and F♮). Starting in **D4**, we have the B♭ (♭3) and then in **D6-7**, the previously unheard ♭5 (D♭). Notice how the first four notes of this phrase are from the G minor pentatonic (a blues version of the G major pentatonic motif), and then how we end the phrase with the inverted chromatic motif (D, D♭, C).

[Play the tenor and trombone parts by themselves, and then together. They are mostly unison, but they go into harmony at crucial points. Now play them with the roots of the chords. There is a rich relationship of dissonance and consonance as well as complexity and simplicity. Listen to the recording. Did the soloist understand the function of the background and respond accordingly? Do we feel ready and eager to hit the shout chorus?]

Shout Chorus

(See *Score* pp. 6-7/pp. 75-76.) Since we've already decided where the tenor plays harmony notes, let's just add the bone on his own pitches, in the same rhythms as the tenor. I have three concerns:

- Overall sonority. Giving the bone an unused note of the chord.
- Intervallic relationships with the other two horns and the bass, creating tension and release.
- Creating a good melody for the trombone.

In order to accomplish all three of the above goals, you may have to do a little juggling. In order to keep the same tone as the head, we can utilize frequent 3rds and 7ths. Let's take a look.

We start out with the 7th on the Bm7, but when we get to the anticipation of the Am7 at the end of **E2**, I opt for the 9th rather than the 7th of the chord. The 9th rubs up against the minor 3rd. These syncopations on the *and-of-2* and the *and-of-4* sound more percussive with half-steps in the voicing. The next note (F#) is the 3rd of the anticipated D7. Since the trumpet has the 6th of G, the tenor has B (the 3rd), and the bass has the root on the *and-of-4* of **E3**, this leaves the 5th (D) for the bone. The G (♭5) on the anticipated C#m7-5 is the characteristic note.

Since the trumpet and tenor are covering the 3rd and 7th of the Bm7 on the downbeat of **E5**, we could give the bone the root or the 5th. I opted for the root—

again, it's a more complex sonority than if I gave the bone the 5th and created a D major triad over B. The following beat stays on the Bm7. The trumpet has the root, and the tenor has the 3rd. This leaves the 7th for the bone.

On the *and*-of-2 the trumpet moves to an A and the tenor to a D♭, the major 7th and 3rd of the anticipated B♭° chord. I opted to give the bone the root (even though the bass is playing the root also), so that the bone and trumpet form the dissonant major 7th interval between root and major 7th.

Beat 4 of **E5** stays on the B♭° with the more conventional 4-part voicing: top down—diminished 5th, diminished 7th, minor 3rd and root (in the bass). This resolves to another 4-part chord—D/A (6, 3, 1, 5). Notice the contrary motion in the bone part moving in and out of the B♭° chord. It's amazing how simple 4-part harmony can sound so rich with a touch of dissonance and contrary motion.

The next two chords (Gm6 and F#m7) have the bone playing the 3rd and 7th respectively. He then moves to the root of the F° and Em7. The tenor has the 7th of the Em7, and the trumpet moves chromatically from the 11th to the 5th. The 11th functions like the 3rd, so I don't want to give the bone the 3rd. The trumpet moves to the 5th, and the tenor has the 7th, so I'll avoid all of them. That leaves the root.

In **E8** the bone covers the 3rd of E♭7+9 and D7+9, and then remains on his F#, which becomes the 7th of A♭7. While I've been discussing the harmonic function of the trombone part, let's not overlook his melody for these eight bars at letter **E**. The line has an interesting shape, and is purely diatonic for four bars before introducing some chromatics for the next four bars, all the while remaining below the tenor part.

Filling in the Missing Harmonies

Letter **F** starts with the bone on the 5th of the tonic G chord because the trumpet and tenor are covering the 3rd and 7th. The rest of **F1-3** has the bone on 3rds and 7ths, much as we've been doing throughout the arrangement. **F4** has the trumpet and tenor in unison. Putting the bone in the same octave as the trumpet will have the bone sound dominate, since the bone is in a stronger register. I wasn't looking to change away from trumpet lead, so I voiced the bone an octave lower than the trumpet/tenor unison. After that, it's all 3rds and 7ths for the rest of letter **F**.

[Let's play the bone part on the piano, and then add the bass. Also play the bone against the trumpet, then the bone against the tenor. After I write a passage, I like to play each individual part against all the other parts. This gives me a good understanding of the internal tension and release. All this knowledge goes into my subconscious, and will help shape the rest of the chart.

Now listen to the recording of the of the shout chorus. Does the development seem logical? It's the arranger's job to tell a compelling story. We don't want to confuse the listener.]

Recap and Coda

The recap is a *D.S.*, so we don't have to write any new material. The Coda (see **Score** p. 8/p. 77) starts with five bars of 3rds and 7ths before we deviate to create the contrary motion in the 6th bar. The B♭ is the 3rd of Gm7. The C is the ♭5 of the F#m7-5 (the characteristic note of a half-diminished chord). Since the trumpet and tenor are covering the 3rd and 7th of the F9 chord, I had the bone continue his line up one more step to the D, which is the 13th of the F9 chord. This is interesting to us not only for the contrary motion that the bone provides, but also for the minor 2nd dissonance against the tenor sax. The last two bars of the chart are much like the last two bars of the head. Don't fix it if it ain't broke.

[Let's listen to the entire chart now. Is there a consistent character to the piece? Does it develop sufficiently to feel satisfying? Notice how much richer the three horns sound compared to the two-horn (quintet) chart. This is a subtle difference, but fun for me as an arranger and listener.

Now, I want you to think about what you liked about this chart—some general things and some specific things. These will be ammunition for when you are writing your own arrangements. Next, think about what you didn't like. How could you change or avoid these situations?]

7. Mary, Even Grander Than That Octet Arrangement (5 Horns)

Now we are going to add two more horns to our sextet arrangement of **Mary**—alto and baritone saxophone. This gives us a little big band: 3 saxes, 2 brass and 3 rhythm. I love this instrumentation, because it offers a wide variety of color and as much as 5-part harmony (or 6-part, if you include the bass). Everyone in the group gets more solo space and is more integral to the ensemble than in a traditional 15 or 16-piece big band. Plus, there is the financial advantage of fewer mouths to feed. A group this size won't have the power, impact, and richness of a big band, but this instrumentation covers a lot of the bases.

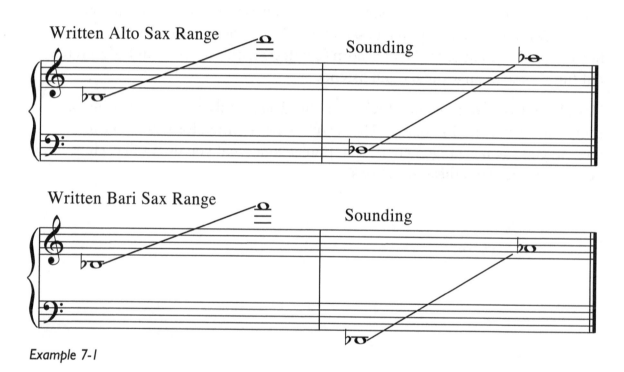

Example 7-1

Orchestrational Tendencies for the Alto and Baritone

Because of their respective ranges, the alto and baritone saxes normally function in the top part of the voicings (alto) or on the bottom (notably, roots in the bari). This is how they function most of the time, but a good orchestrator will make use of the entire range of each instrument. Sometimes the alto is effective in the low register, and the baritone can sing on the top notes.

Thirds and Sevenths

Both instruments are very useful playing the color notes of the chords (3rds and 7ths). However, in this arrangement, because I have already assigned those pitches to the tenor and trombone (and in a few instances, the trumpet), I need to find other uses for the alto and bari. The bari was easy.

Putting the Baritone on the Roots of the Chords

In this chart, the baritone mostly plays the roots of the chords deep in the bass clef. This gives the ensemble greater depth and weight, making it appear to be larger than its octet size. With the exception of unisons, inversions, and voicings where the root appears in an inner voice, I've assigned the bari roots on the bottom.

What Notes to Assign the Alto Sax

Normally in a group this size, the alto sax plays in unison with the trumpet or plays the harmony note just below the trumpet. This holds true for this arrangement. There are a number of voicings where I only wanted four different pitches. Since there are five horns, I had the choice of either doubling the trumpet melody in the alto sax or doubling the trumpet note an octave lower, either in the bari sax or in one of the other voices. Since the tenor and bone were already written and don't include any doubling of the trumpet notes, I opted to double the alto with the trumpet. Another reason, and actually the primary reason for doubling the alto and trumpet, is to soften the brightness of the trumpet lead sound, so that it blends more with the other horns. (See *Score* and pp. 86-93).

Listening to Bird and Miles

I grew up listening to Charlie Parker's recordings, so many of which have the melodies played by trumpet and alto in unison. They combine to create a light, flexible sound associated with bebop. Miles Davis' *Birth Of The Cool* recordings utilized that doubling with Miles in unison with Lee Konitz. Those arrangements were mostly written or influenced by Gil Evans, whose approach can be heard in the other arrangers on those sides.

Introduction

Scoring the Baritone Part

As I just said, I'm going to keep the trumpet, tenor, and trombone parts intact, and add the alto on or near the top, and give the bari primarily the roots at the bottom. Right away, the bari's first 4 notes are the roots of the chord (see *Score* p. 1/p. 86).

Adding the Alto

Writing the alto part is going to take a bit more thought. The alto starts in unison with the trumpet for the first 3½ beats. When the trumpet ascends to the A, the alto remains on the E, and joins with the other horns and rhythm section. The alto's E is the ♭5 of the B♭° chord. This note was missing from the 3-horn voicing. In general, with four or five horns, we want to create complete 4- or 5-note voicings in the horns. We couldn't do this before, with fewer than four horns, but complete voicings add a richness that we now expect. Also, adding the missing note in the voicings helps us to avoid awkward unison doublings and octave doublings in the horns.

Proceeding with giving the alto the missing chord tones, he stays on the E, which becomes the 5th of the Am7. Rather than sticking with the E one more time, I had him slide up chromatically to the F♮, which is the 13th of the A♭7-5 chord. The F gives him a more satisfying line while creating a dissonant major 7th with the F# in the trombone. Notice how the alto and the bone move into that dissonance in contrary motion.

A Holdover from Vocal Arranging

When writing for singers, arrangers learn quickly that it is difficult for singers to hear the dissonant intervals of ♭2nd, major 7th, and ♭9th. If we approach them in contrary or oblique motion, they are much easier to sing. Although instrumentalists don't have this same limitation, I've come to love the sound of dissonances approached this way. Of course, I still write parallel dissonant voicings at times, but mostly, I reserve that for planing (completely parallel voicings) or constant structures.

The Head

(See *Score* pp. 2-3/pp. 87-88.) I stopped coupling the alto with the trumpet at the bar before **A**. For the next 2 bars, the alto joins the rhythm section and other horns to answer the trumpet. The bari is on the roots, and the tenor and bone have 3rds and 7ths. This leaves the alto to play 9ths, 11ths and 13ths. In **A1** he has the 9th on the F7 and the +9 on the E7. I like how he repeats his pitches while the bass and the other horns move. This same situation occurs a bar later on the Bm11 and B♭7-5, except that now the trumpet finally joins up with the alto on the final E (the ♭5 on the B♭7). Going back to **A1**, the alto is the only horn acting with the bass in answering the trumpet on the *and*-of-3. They form a tritone between the root and the ♭5. This is a bit quirky, but sets up the baritone sax/bass unison answer in the following bar (**A2**).

Bari Roots and Alto/Trumpet Unison leading to Call-and-Response

As promised in the intro, **A3-6** is all bari on the roots of the chords, and the alto doubling the trumpet at the unison. The turnaround in **A7-8** returns to the call-and-response pattern, similar to **A1-2**. However, this time, the tenor is playing tensions in **A6**, which leaves the 3rd of E♭9 and the 7th of A♭9+5 open for the alto to cover. I had the alto dip down below the tenor and bone into the low register, to cover those pitches. This is a bit unusual, but there are numerous examples in Duke Ellington's and Sy Oliver's charts where the order in the reeds is switched. The alto's low register will sound grittier than the tenor, and the tenor on the higher notes will have less bite than the alto. Things go back to normal a bar later in **A8**. As in **A1**, the alto plays the 9th of F7 and the +9 of E7 before ending the phrase with the ♭5 of the E♭7-5 chord.

Setting the Tone

Notice how easy and logical it is to write the alto and bari parts, once the formula has been set up in the intro. This is the basic tone for the entire arrangement. Unlike big band and orchestra charts, which have a large palette and scope, small group charts are miniatures that are designed mostly as showcases for the soloists.

Come Sopra

B1-3 is a *come sopra* of measures **A1-3**. That means an exact copy "as before." In our computer age, we call this "copy and paste." **B4** has the trumpet and alto in unison. Then they break into harmony for two bars at **B5-6**. The alto picks up tensions 13, ♭9 and 13 in **B5** and then chord tones 5, 5, and 3 in **B6**. On the F7-5, the alto plays the 9th and then on the *and*-of-4, moves to the ♭9 to be alone with the trumpet in 3rds.

Combining Unison and Harmony

An interesting situation arises in **B7**. The trumpet has two escape tones (A and B). This is an opportunity to be creative texturally by having the alto play the unison E on the downbeat and hold it, while the trumpet jumps up to the A, the non-harmonic major 7th on the B♭7. The alto then moves to the F# in unison with the trumpet. This time, when the trumpet jumps to the escape tone (B), everyone is voiced below him in an A♭7-9 chord with the alto on the +5. The alto and trumpet resolve to the tonic in unison on the *and*-of-4. There is no need for the alto to join the leading tone amen in **B8**. It's more effective to leave it triadic.

[Play the bari part with the trumpet part on the piano. Since the bari contains the roots in unison with the bass (with the exception of the Em7 chord in **A6**, where the bone has the root, and the bari plays the 5th), this should all sound as solid as it did when we first wrote the bass part. Now play the alto and bari parts together, and then the alto and the trumpet together. Strong intervallic relationships between parts gives the music structure and shapes the players' experience. They feel secure, and at times, challenged. When there is tension, it is resolved before they lose faith in the arranger.]

Solos

(See *Score* pp. 4-5/pp. 89-90.) The mostly unison background needs to be soft and light. For that reason, I put the alto and the baritone in the same register as the bone and tenor. When writing alto/bari unisons, there is always the choice of absolute unison or octave unison. Octaves are natural, since the bari has twice the length of the alto, but octaves have more weight. So if the line doesn't go above

CJCA III: WRITING FOR SMALL GROUPS

Example 7-2 *Mary's A Grand Old Name* octet score, page 1

Example 7-2 Mary's A Grand Old Name octet score, page 2

CJCA III: WRITING FOR SMALL GROUPS

Example 7-2 Mary's A Grand Old Name octet score, page 3

Example 7-2 *Mary's A Grand Old Name* octet score, page 4

CJCA III: WRITING FOR SMALL GROUPS

Example 7-2 *Mary's A Grand Old Name* octet score, page 5

MARY – OCTET ARRANGEMENT

Example 7-2 *Mary's A Grand Old Name* octet score, page 6

CJCA III: WRITING FOR SMALL GROUPS

Example 7-2 Mary's A Grand Old Name octet score, page 7

MARY – OCTET ARRANGEMENT

Example 7-2 *Mary's A Grand Old Name* octet score, page 8

Unison and 4-Part Close

With that in mind, **C1-7** has the 4-horn background in absolute unison. When we go into harmony at **C8**, the tenor has the top part, and the bone has the bottom. I put the alto and the bari in the middle of the voicing playing a m2 interval (3/9 on the Am7 and 7/13 on the D7). These notes added to the tenor and bari create 4-part close harmony. This is the only time this occurs in the entire arrangement.

A Tad More Unison—This is Just a Tease

The pickups to **D** and the downbeat of **D** are all in unison. This is an interesting situation. The harmony here is D7 to G, so the bass goes D to G while the horns all play the opposite (repeated Gs resolving to D on the downbeat).

Plain and Sophisticated Open Harmony

On beat 3 of **D1**, we go into open harmony with the bari on the roots. Remember our old chromatic motif (D, D#, E)? It returns here in the alto lead part before returning to the starting G and D (this time descending, rather than ascending). The D# forms the 7th of the F7 chord voiced from the bottom up: 1, 5, 3, 7. That's right—no tensions. It's a plain old F7.

I don't know if you were trained to be prejudiced against 7th chords with no tensions, but I certainly was. They can sound so unsophisticated. But sometimes, and this is one of those times, they sound very sophisticated, and adding a tension would spoil the moment. The same can be true with triads. It took me years to learn this. You should have heard my early charts... every chord had 13 different pitches in it!

When I was in college, I took a choral arranging course with Mary Ann Covert. She was also my theory teacher, so I already knew that she knew what she was talking about. I wrote a chart for the college choir on the Kurt Weill/Ira Gershwin standard, *My Ship*. Every note in the entire chart was in 7-part harmony. When I showed it to Mrs. Covert (women were Miss or Mrs. then), she played through the entire chart, without saying a word. When she got to the end, she said, "You know, if every chord is dissonant, the dissonance becomes consonance." After letting that rattle around my brain for a few years, I came to realize that the same thing is true of all extremes. Not only do they wear out their welcome, but they become the norm and lose their power. It's like people who swear all the time.

Open Voicings Implying Tritone Subs

In **D2-3**, the bari plays the root of Bm7 and Am7 and the ♭5 of the E7 and D7, implying the tritone substitutes B♭7 and A♭7. The reason I chose to put the ♭5 on the bottom is to avoid the octave doubling with the alto part playing the E and D roots on the top of the voicing. Also the bari's descending chromatics are the inversion of our chromatic motif. On the Bm7 the alto has the 11th and on the Am7 the 7th.

Flat 9ths on Tritone Subs

The alto and bari join in the unison with the tenor and bari for **D4-6** and split into harmony for the E♭7 and D7. The E♭7 is really a tritone sub for A7. My teacher, Ray Wright, used to say, "No flat 9ths on tritone subs." However, when I occasionally wrote one, he would tell me that it was okay. So what's the deal? You want to avoid the parallel downward resolution of the m9 interval between the ♭9 and the root. If the ♭9 resolves upward (contrary motion) or stays on the same pitch (oblique motion), we can justify the temporary dissonance. In **D7**, the alto repeats the E (first as the ♭9 on E♭7 and then as the 9th on the D7. The horns then duck out and let the rhythm section play the chromatic turnaround by themselves—more use of the chromatic motif.

Shout Chorus

(See *Score* pp. 6-7/pp. 91-92.) In keeping with the orchestration of the rest of the chart, the bari will continue to play the roots of the chords, and the alto will alternate between unison with the trumpet and providing either a missing harmony note or adding a tension to create a little spice.

Exceptions in the Bari

Although the bari is consigned almost exclusively to roots in this chart, there are a few spots where he deviates. In **E3** on the *and*-of-2, he plays the ♭5 of the D7 chord. The D root sounds a bit vanilla and the A♭ provides the middle note of the inverted chromatic motif. I love when melodic motifs appear on the inside or bottom voices. It's all part of the integrity of the piece, like foreground becoming background and vice versa, as we saw in our background for the solo section of this chart.

The bari also abandons the roots for the first and third notes in **E5**. In both of those chords, the root appears in one of the other horn parts, so the bari plays the 5th of the Bm7 and the ♭5 of the B♭°. Similarly in the next bar **E6**, the bari plays the 5th of the D/A in octaves with the bass, the 11th of the F#m7, and the °7 of the F°. The 11th of the F#m7 came about from my desire not to double the root that appears in the trumpet part. We are going along nicely with no octave doublings in the horns, so I didn't want to suddenly introduce that sound.

An interesting situation occurs in **E7**. The trombone and bari play the E root in unison so that the bari can then gliss down to the A on the 3rd beat. The Em7/A is functionally an A7sus4 chord. After that, the bari sticks with the roots of the chords with the exception of **E4**, where all the horns are in octave unison.

Adding the Alto Sax Part

Since this chart already sounds complete without the alto, I'm either going to find him a fifth pitch, or put him in unison with the trumpet. Adding a fifth note should be done with care. I don't like cluttering up the voicings. With that in mind, **E1-5** has the alto in unison with the trumpet until the beat 4 of **E5**, where the alto sounds a C (the 9th of the B♭°). I like the major 7th interval between the alto and the bone. It adds just a little spice for a moment, before returning to unison with the trumpet on the next note (the 6th of the D/A). Since there is no 5th in the following Gm6 chord, the alto jumps down to the D and then jumps back up to the C# to fill in the missing 5th of the F#m7 chord.

Voice Leading

OK, I know what you're thinking—how are those two large leaps in the alto good voice leading? Actually, that is a good question. When we leap down to the D, the alto crosses over the tenor, creating a bit of confusion. Leaping up to the C# helps to support, and even to focus our attention on this leap to the highest note in the trumpet part. This is the climax of the chart. We want to bring attention to it with something special.

Back to Unison

After that, the alto joins the trumpet in unison until **E8**, where the alto adds +9s to the E♭7 and the D7 before adding the ♭5 to the A♭7 chords. Notice that although the chord change for the third beat of **E8** is D7, I voiced the *and* of that beat as an A♭7, giving us three A♭7 voicings in a row. Had I voiced the *and*-of-3 as a D7, that would have broken up the continuity of this repetitive pickup to letter **F**.

Change vs. Repetition

One of the major opposites that we must always balance in our music is change and repetition. The more the music stays the same (through repetition), the more groove. But at a certain point, we catch on—and stop listening. We know what is coming next, so there is no need to pay attention. Just before that happens, we need to change to something different. This is exactly what we do when we tell a joke. That surprise coming at the exact moment when the listener assumes what is next, is what makes us laugh.

This is our game. Some music is highly repetitive, and for that reason, it probably isn't going to sustain our listening attention, but it may make good dance music or film music, where listening is a secondary consideration.

The danger of writing too much change (surprise) in your music, is that listeners feel constantly outsmarted and become frustrated. Ultimately, they give up. Also, the more change, the less groove. There needs to be a workable balance, or your music has little chance of reaching a wide audience.

Pop music is highly repetitive. It can attract a wide audience, but only for a short time, before they move on to something else.

More Moving In and Out of Unison

Letter **F** has the alto alternating between unison with the trumpet and playing a harmony note. **F1-4** is all unison, except for the downbeat for **F2** when the alto jumps down to fill in the missing 7th of the Bm7-5. Similarly, in **F5** the alto plays the missing 7th of the Bm7, and then adds the 9th of the B♭7-5. A similar situation happens a bar later, but this time the alto provides the missing 5th of the Bm7 before adding the 9th to the B♭7-5. Then it's back to unison. In **F8** the alto stays in unison with the trumpet except for the trumpet's escape tone on the *and*-of-1. This is a nice reminder of the escape tones way back in **B7**.

[Once again, play the alto part for the shout chorus against all the other parts and hear how they interact. Would this be a part you would want to play? One of the joys of playing in an ensemble is experiencing the feeling of how your part fits in with the other parts.

About 25 years ago, when we were on the road performing *Harlem Nutcracker* eight shows per week, trombonist Art Baron told me one day how much he enjoyed playing a subtle little passage in the show. He started the measure a half-step below Britt Woodman, and by the third beat, he had moved down to a half-step above Wayne Goodman. This measure repeated a few times. It's not often that players tell arrangers about specific things they like in their parts, so it's nice to hear that the details that we embed in our arrangements don't go unnoticed.]

D.S. and Coda

The *D.S.* has no changes. The bari plays roots throughout. The first bar of the coda is identical to **B5**. The third bar of the coda (see *Score* p. 8/p. 93) is similar. The alto plays the 13th of the D7 and then descends chromatically along with the bass and in contrary motion to the trumpet. The alto then adds the 9th to the next four chords: F7, Bm7, Am7 and Gm7. On the F#m7-5, the alto fills in the missing minor 3rd. On the F7, he adds the 9th before joining the trumpet in unison for the last 8th note of the bar. The final two bars of the chart are identical to **B7-8** (the final two bars of the head).

[Play the alto part on the coda against the other parts. In order to build to a satisfying conclusion, I've expanded the harmony to a consistent five parts, giving the alto 9ths and 13ths. Note how the drum interjections give us a moment to digest the harmonies. Now go back and listen to the entire chart. How much do the alto and baritone add? Think about fullness, weight, and integration of reeds and brass.

I'm going to recommend a little listening. My old buddy, Rod Levitt, had an octet in the 1960s. After working with Dizzy Gillespie and Gil Evans, Rod spent the rest of his career writing hundreds of jingles, although he once confessed to me that he really had no idea what made people buy a certain brand of toilet paper. Rod recorded four octet records back then, and they are all gems:

- *The Dynamic Sound Patterns of the Rod Levitt Orchestra* (Riverside Records, 1964)
- *Insight* (RCA Victor, 1965)
- *Solid Ground* (RCA Victor, 1966)
- *Forty-Second Street* (RCA Victor, 1966)

His love of Ellington is quite apparent, but you'll hear all kinds of influences, not least of which is Igor Stravinsky. The main thing that I learned from Rod's music was the importance of personality in the individual voices and writing good lines for everyone.]

8. The Silver Bullet
Octet Arrangement

This original of mine is dedicated to Horace Silver, the master composer and arranger for the jazz quintet. In 1961, when I was 12 years old and fell in love with jazz, the first jazz record I bought was *Horace Silver and the Jazz Messengers*. I think the main reason I bought it was that it had the first (and seminal) recording of Horace's tunes, *The Preacher*, which became a hit in 1961, and *Doodlin'*. Although I loved *The Preacher* and *Doodlin'* (and still do), I listened to the entire record over and over until I knew every single note and nuance. Kenny Dorham, Hank Mobley, Art Blakey, and, of course, Horace became like gods to me. This was jazz. This is what I wanted to do with my life.

As I write this book over 60 years later, I realize that many readers consider *Horace Silver and the Jazz Messengers* a classic record—and, like the classical music of Beethoven and Mozart, nearly prehistoric—from the remote past. But when I bought it and first listened to it, those sides were only a few years old. Horace was constantly on jazz radio stations with a seemingly unending stream of great new records containing his new jazz standards that we young jazz players all learned and played.

Unfortunately, I never got to work with Horace. I met him only twice. The first time was in the mid-1970s. I was a young trumpet player in New York and was dating a cute NYU student who, it turned out, was taking a jazz appreciation class. One day she invited me to an upcoming class where Horace Silver was to be the guest speaker. I had seen Horace perform at the Village Vanguard several times. Several of my buddies worked with him around that time, but I was too shy to ask them to introduce me. Seeing Horace off the bandstand was a new experience. I wanted to know how he did what he did.

Horace had a new record out, *The Sophisticated Hippie*, which was dedicated to Duke Ellington. I had heard the record on the radio and it didn't sound like Ellington to me. In that class, Horace played a cut from the record and after a brief discussion, opened it up for questions. I waited for the students to go first, and then I asked Horace, "Aside from the obvious piano influence of Bud Powell, who were your influences as a composer?" To which, Horace answered, "Only one—Duke Ellington." I was flabbergasted. I told him that I couldn't hear it. He assured me that he was telling the truth.

Our paths didn't cross for another 30 years, until I ran into him at a jazz educators' convention. I always feel awkward approaching people that I don't know, but I knew that this would probably be the last opportunity I would ever have to speak to him—he had recently retired and begun to slip into dementia. So, I introduced myself, told him that I was his biggest fan, and told him of our previous meeting, which he understandably had no memory of. Then I told him that it had taken me 30 years, but I now understood the relationship of his music to Ellington's. I thanked him for his music and for inspiring me. All this took about three or four minutes, and then we parted. I have no idea if what I said meant anything to him. After all, millions of people all over the world loved his music, but it meant a lot to me to thank him. The gratitude I have felt and still feel toward him is immeasurable.

I don't often set out to pay specific homage in my music to other jazz composers and arrangers, but I have written three compositions with Horace in mind. Two of them are included in this book. The third is *The Rising Storm*, a big band chart that is analyzed in **Creative Jazz Composing and Arranging, Vol. 1** (available from **www.suchsweetthundermusic.com**).

I didn't want to copy anything specifically of Horace's in **The Silver Bullet**, but just to get his playful vibe and hip chromatic changes. The title invokes not only Horace's last name (something he frequently did when titling his own music), but also a radio, TV, and movie reference.

When I was a little kid, I watched *The Lone Ranger* on TV religiously. This masked man fought for justice in the Old West. His horse's name was Silver. Another TV cowboy of my childhood was Roy Rogers, whose dog was named Bullet, but the reference here is that the Lone Ranger shot at outlaws with silver bullets. Although in the TV series and movie *Lone Ranger* was played by a white man, Clayton Moore, I learned many years later that the true historical Lone Ranger was a Black man, which was very unusual for a Texas Ranger in the 19th century.

The movie reference is to *Dr. Ehrlich's Magic Bullet*, starring Edward G. Robinson, about (German Nobel laureate Paul) Ehrlich's fight to find a cure for syphilis against the public's desire to keep everything related to sex illegal and shameful. It's always been easier for me to address uncomfortable issues in my music than in words or actions.

Introduction

Unlike most of my charts, the initial impetus for this piece was the introduction. I started writing at the top, and then kept going—curious to see where it would lead (see *Score* p. 1/p. 106). In the back of my mind, I reserved the right to 86 the intro if, in the end, it was misleading or not enough of a tease.

Re-using the Intro

The result in this instance is that the intro is so strong, I reused it, following the end of the head, as a send-off to the first solo. It also comes back at the start of the recapitulation (the *D.S.*), and then again after the recap as a coda or outro. I can't really hear this tune without the intro. In fact, I might analyze the form of the tune (including the intro) as *abcba*, rather than *Intro aba Intro*. Since the intro appears as the fourth section solo section (*aba intro*), the analysis could go either way.

aba Form

The *aba* form is a bit unusual in jazz. When we say *aba* form, we generally mean *aaba*, but this tune doesn't repeat the *a* section until after the bridge. I didn't set out to do this; it just seemed natural to move on to the bridge at **B**. This could have signaled an *abac* form, which, if you consider the intro as *c*, I suppose it is, but c sections don't normally show their face before the first statement of *a*. I've written thousands of charts and hundreds of original tunes, but never encountered this form before or since. All I can say is that it feels right to me—sometimes it just be's that way.

Writing Out Piano Voicings

Unlike my chart on *Mary*, the piano acts in call-and-response with the horns. I wrote out specific piano voicings rather than just giving the pianist chord changes. I definitely want to hear these exact voicings every time we perform this chart—it's part of the composition. Any other voicings would diminish the relationship between the horn voicings and the piano voicings.

Dynamic Use of Space

Note that the piano only plays four chords in this intro. There is no need to double the horn voicings, and the use of space draws our ear to the statement that the piano makes in the intro as well as what follows at **A** and **B**. If the piano comps all the time, we tend to tune it out.

Voicing Up in 3rds

The way I learned to voice chords was to put the root on the bottom and then add voices on top with a 3rd between each voice. This is basic stuff, but can still sound great in the appropriate context. I often use it when voicing saxes and brass, but as we can hear right from the first note of this chart, this method of voicing can also be effective for piano. Mostly, I use more open voicings for piano, but this is what I was hearing. The root is at the bottom of the bass clef (in unison with the bassist), and then I built 3rds, starting a 10th above the root: F#m11 to Gm11. It's simple: 1, 3, 5, 7, 9, 11.

Motivic Development

The two motifs for this chart occur in the first two notes horizontally and vertically. These are the aforementioned vertical 3rds and the horizontal ascending chromatic minor 2nd. The entire voicing moves up by half-step. Everything that happens from then on is either 3rds or minor 2nds, so you can understand why these piano voicings are essential to the meaning of the entire chart.

Call-and-Response

The trumpet and alto answer the piano chords with a horizontal (melodic) version of the motifs. They start with an ascending half-step and then arpeggiate up the Gm9 in 3rds. The pattern repeats, but instead of a short eighth note on the 9th, the trumpet holds out the 9th for a dotted quarter before resolving down a half-step to another long note. This second long note needs to be more interesting than its predecessor, so I syncopate it and give it an altered dominant voicing in the horns.

Unison Pickups Resolving to a Harmonized Downbeat

When notes are going by quickly, we can keep things light and support the forward motion by making those notes unison, rather than voicing them out. This is what happens in bar **1** when we arpeggiate up the Gm9 chord twice beginning with the upward half-step from the 9th to the 3rd.

What key are we in?

Bar **1**'s Gm9 remains for the first beat and a half of bar **2** before resolving to C7-9+5. This appears to be *ii V* in F, but let's not jump to conclusions until we resolve to a tonic.

When the long notes appear in bar **2**, I voice out both chords in the five horns. The first one is a Gm9 voiced in Drop 2, with an added root on the bottom. That moves smoothly to a C7-9+5. Each voice moves down by half-step or stays on the same pitch except for the roots on the bottom, which move up a perfect 4th. I could have had the bari and the bassist move down chromatically to a G♭, which would go along with our chromatic motif, but I felt that would be too much sameness. We need some resistance. The contrary motion moving up from G to C fights the descending chromatic motion going on above it. The insistent B♭s in the trombone offer a weaker but welcome stasis.

So Nice, Let's Do It Twice

Measures **3** and **4** are identical to **1** and **2**, except down a half-step—again, our minor 2nd motif at work. When I try that one more time in measure **5**, I need to go somewhere else because, by now, you've figured out my game. This is where things get complicated.

The basic harmonic scheme for the intro is Gm9 for 5½ beats followed by C7-9+5 for 2½ beats, the same pattern down a half-step (G♭m9 C♭7-9+5), and then Fm9 for 5 beats followed by C♭13, B♭9-5, B♭7-9+5 for a beat a piece, a bar of E♭69+11, and finally Fm7 moving up in half-steps in quarter notes in the eighth bar. The final chord (A♭m7) leads chromatically up to the Am7 on the first beat of letter **A**.

Notice how the descending *ii V* patterns of measures **1-4** are answered first by a *ii V* with an inserted chromatic *♭VI* to *V* in bar **6** and then finally the satisfying opposite of chromatic ascending *ii* chords. What goes up, must come down. We crave it.

Flavor

The overriding flavor of this piece is the bland, middle class *iim7* chord moving to the dark, complex *V* dominant 7th chord with altered tensions (-9 and +5). This is set up in the intro and developed in the *a* section (letter **A**). In order to avoid repetition of roots in the bari, I have him jumping octaves, so that sometimes his root is on the bottom of the voicing, and sometimes he is in the middle and rubs in half-steps with the ♭9 just above him. This half-step is the appeal for me. Had there not been this minor 2nd between the root and ♭9, I would have looked for another solution—a different voicing, different chord, or possibly a different melody note.

One More Once

Bar **5** is the same as bar **3**, except down a half-step, so, it looks as if we are going to repeat the same pattern as we did in bars **3-4** repeating **1-2** down a half-step. That seems too predictable to me, so I change course in midstream. Bar **6** gets four quarter notes, which extend the opening two chromatic quarter notes to four notes. The first two melody notes are the upward chromatic but reharmonized. The next three quarters are *sol, re, do* in A major (the tritone sub of our key of E♭). To draw our attention to the important tonic resolution, I've expanded the descending half-step pattern to a descending whole step (B♮ to A—*re do*).

Obscuring the Perfect Cadence Even More

When we finally get to our *V I* cadence, the A♮ melody note not only functions as the tonic of A major, but also as the +11 of E♭69 (the tritone sub of A). We get to that tonic chord by *ii V* (Fm9 B♭9-5 B♭7-9+5). I stuck a B13 between the Fm9 and B♭9-5 to harmonize the G# melody note. The B13 resolves down to the B♭9-5 by half-step. We're still in the intro, and we've heard a pile of half-step resolutions, both melodically and harmonically. This gives the piece a certain personality.

What Goes Up Must Come Down

The descending arpeggio in the last two beats of bar **7** satisfies our need for the opposite of all the previous ascending arpeggios. It's a simple Gm arpeggio, which both functions as the triad built on the 3rd of the E♭maj7 chord and relates back to the opening Gm9 arpeggio in measure **1**. It's nice when things come back.

Upper and Lower Neighbors

The triplet turn on beat 2 of bar **7** uses the diatonic upper neighbor to C (major 6th, major 7th, major 6th) before returning to the A♮, which now functions as a chromatic lower neighbor to the B♭ (5th of the E♭maj7). This gesture can be heard as an embellished enclosure of the B♭. Although this piece is primarily about chromatic (half-step) movement, I've sprinkled in a few whole steps to make things less predictable. These three beats are played by the trumpet and alto in unison, to give this little throwaway figure less weight.

More Ascending Half-Steps

Measure **8** consists of four quarter notes in ascending half-steps: Fm7 F#m7 Gm7 G#m7, leading to an Am7 on the downbeat of letter **A**. Notice that there are only four pitches in each voicing for the five horns. I didn't want to add a 9th or 11th to these chords. They sound better in their pure form. Rather than having one of the horns rest for this measure, I doubled the trumpet with the alto sax on the top note. This gives us continuity from the trumpet/alto unisons in bars **1**, **3**, **5**, and **7**.

Big Stuff

The most important aspect of the intro is the stop time pattern in the rhythm section. When we go into 2 with the drummer on the hi-hat at **A**, this clearly delineates the form; we've gone from the intro to the head. Although the intro lays out the quarter note and half-step motives in addition to the *iim7 V7-9+5* harmonic coloration which will all occur in a somewhat different guise at **A**, the move from stop time to 2-beat outweighs everything else. We may not consciously notice it, but we certainly feel it.

The Head

The *a* Section

The *a* section (letter **A**, see p. 107) consists of two identical 4-bar phrases, with the second one a half-step lower than the first. This picks up the chromatically descending 2-bar phrases of the intro using augmentation. The opening quarter notes of the intro reappear at **A**, first with the piano downbeat and then in the successive quarter notes in the horns—9 syncopations, a syncopated dotted quarter, and then three on-the-beat quarters.

Each pair of these syncopated quarter notes is made up of a descending half-step in the top part harmonized with dominant -9+5 chords resolving to minor 9th chords. **A4** finally settles in E♭ major using the stride piano walking pattern *I ii #ii iii*. Where the old stride players used a *#iio*, I kept the constant structure of chromatic minor 7th chords reminiscent of Thelonious Monk. As in the eighth bar of the intro, I used plain minor 7th chords doubling the top part with the trumpet and alto. **A8**, rather than following the previous pattern and cadencing in D, has the surprise B♭m7-5 resolving to E♭7-9. The ascending chromatic F# to G in the trombone and tenor (inside the voicing) inverts the previous descending melodic half-steps.

The *b* Section

At **B** (see *Score* p. 3/p. 108) the rhythm section goes into 4 with the bassist walking and the drummer switching to the ride cymbal, while the horns change their texture from concerted 4- and 5-part harmony to alto/bari octave unison.

The Rhythm Section

I don't need to write specific notes for the piano, bass, and drums. I want to leave it up to them to create their own parts in a stylistically appropriate way. The spontaneity of improvised rhythm section parts contributes mightily to the feeling of jazz.

Contrasting Chord Changes

While the *a* section is an original chromatic chord progression, the *b* section has a more typical Tin Pan Alley chord progression. So many standards and jazz standards have bridges that start on the subdominant and cycle back to the tonic through the *V/ii* and *ii V*. It's essential for the harmonies of the bridge to be as opposite from the *a* section as possible. Also, it's very effective if there is a big change in the harmonic rhythm. Think of *I Got Rhythm*—the *a* section is two beats per change, and the bridge is two measures per change. In **The Silver Bullet** the *a* section is two beats per change, and then the bridge is basically a measure or two per change.

Unison Horn Writing

Unisons create an impersonal approach. By placing the alto and bari in octaves, each is in the same relative place on their instruments—playing the same fingerings with the same overtones. This gets a natural blend. I didn't include the tenor, because he would be in a different register of his instrument, and thus would add a bit more weight and detract slightly from the homogeneous octave sound of the alto and bari.

CJCA III: WRITING FOR SMALL GROUPS

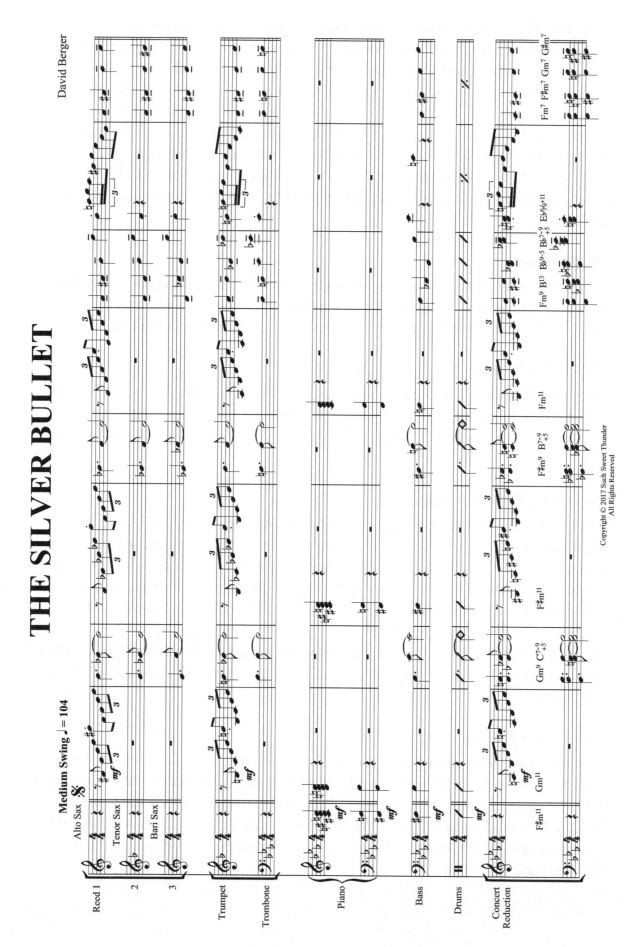

Example 8-1 *The Silver Bullet* octet score, page 1

THE SILVER BULLET – OCTET ARRANGEMENT

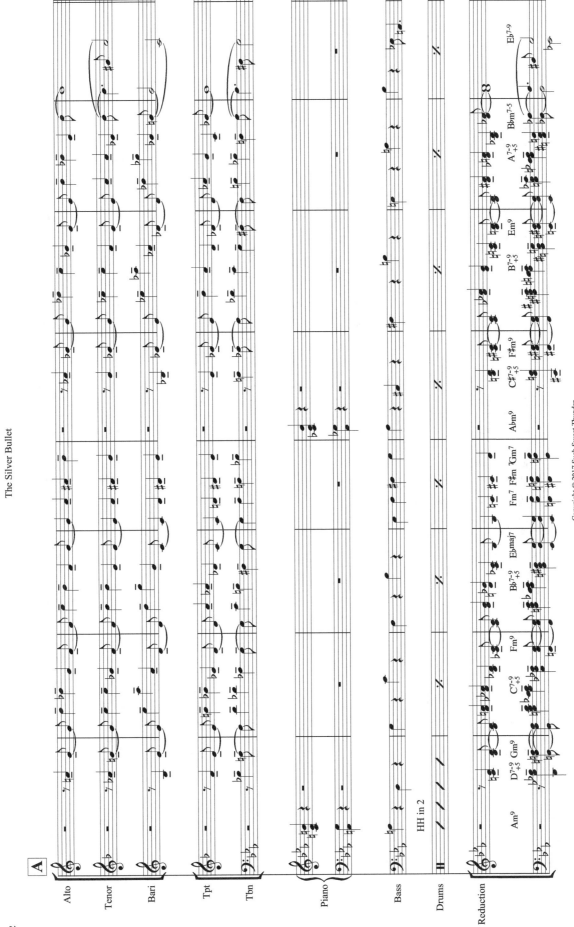

Example 8-1 *The Silver Bullet* octet score, page 2

CJCA III: WRITING FOR SMALL GROUPS

Example 8-1 *The Silver Bullet* octet score, page 3

THE SILVER BULLET – OCTET ARRANGEMENT

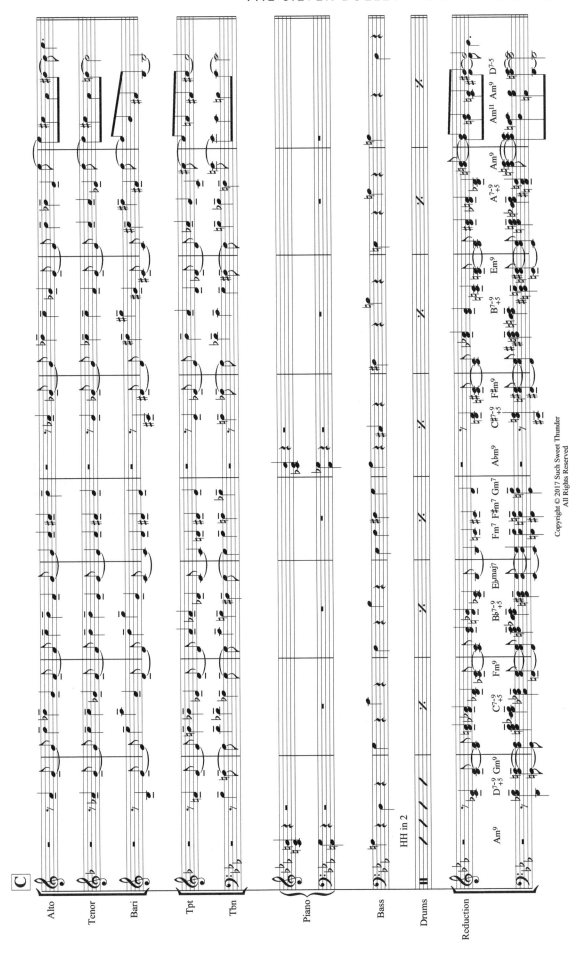

Example 8-1 *The Silver Bullet* octet score, page 4

CJCA III: WRITING FOR SMALL GROUPS

Example 8-1 The Silver Bullet octet score, page 5

THE SILVER BULLET – OCTET ARRANGEMENT

Example 8-1 *The Silver Bullet* octet score, page 6

CJCA III: WRITING FOR SMALL GROUPS

The Silver Bullet

Example 8-1 *The Silver Bullet* octet score, page 7

Alto	F	Fm⁷ Bb⁷	C	Am⁷ D⁷	Dm⁷ G⁷			
Tenor	Bb	Bbm⁷ Eb⁷	F	Dm⁷ G⁷	Gm⁷ C⁷			
Bari	F	Fm⁷ Bb⁷	C	Am⁷ D⁷	Dm⁷ G⁷			
Tpt	Bb	Bbm⁷ Eb⁷	F	Dm⁷ G⁷	Gm⁷ C⁷			
Tbn	Ab	Abm⁷ Db⁷	Eb	Cm⁷ F⁷	Fm⁷ Bb⁷			
Piano	Ab	Abm⁷ Db⁷	Eb	Cm⁷ F⁷	Fm⁷ Bb⁷			
Bass	Ab	Abm⁷ Db⁷	Eb	Cm⁷ F⁷	Fm⁷ Bb⁷			
Drums								
Reduction								

Copyright © 2017 Such Sweet Thunder
All Rights Reserved

THE SILVER BULLET – OCTET ARRANGEMENT

Example 8-1 *The Silver Bullet* octet score, page 8

CJCA III: WRITING FOR SMALL GROUPS

Example 8-1 The Silver Bullet octet score, page 9

THE SILVER BULLET – OCTET ARRANGEMENT

Example 8-1 *The Silver Bullet* octet score, page 10

CJCA III: WRITING FOR SMALL GROUPS

Example 8-1 *The Silver Bullet* octet score, page 11

THE SILVER BULLET – OCTET ARRANGEMENT

Example 8-1 *The Silver Bullet* octet score, page 12

CJCA III: WRITING FOR SMALL GROUPS

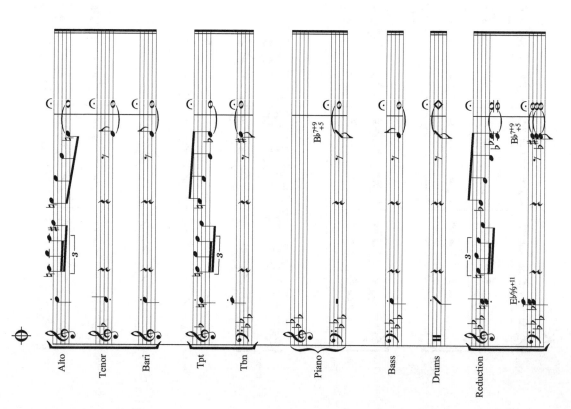

Example 8-1 *The Silver Bullet* octet score, page 13

Expanding the Chromatics

The unison line at **B** (see *Score* p. 3/p. 108) starts with an ascending whole step—expanding the half-step motif slightly. I stick with this by going from the major 7th to the major 6th of the A♭ chord. Where the *a* section moved in quarter notes, the bridge is basically eighth notes.

Moving into the Next Chord Change by Half-step

After the three pairs of whole steps (ascending, descending, ascending), we arpeggiate up the A♭maj7, but instead of landing on the expected root (A♭) or 9th (B♭), surprise! We switch direction and resolve chromatically down to G♭ which becomes the 7th of A♭m7. This is similar to the first three bars of *On Green Dolphin Street*. Switching from the major mode to the minor mode can be most effective. It's no wonder composers have been doing it for hundreds of years.

Making the Subdominant Minor into a *ii V*

The A♭m7 resolves down a 5th to D♭7 (♭*VII7* in E♭) before resolving back to E♭ in **B3**. This *ii V* is a favorite bebop progression. Once we land on the tonic (E♭), we can move the bass down a 3rd to the *vi* chord (Cm7). This is very normal stuff. Then we can move around the circle of 5ths to F9 and B♭7-5. The Fm7 is the *ii* preparation to the B♭7 *V* chord and is approached chromatically from below with an Em7.

The Opposing Bridge

The *b* section or bridge of a tune needs to be as different as possible from the *a* section, while still developing previous material. Let's see if that happens here. **B2** starts with a descending B major arpeggio (7, 5, 3) of the A♭m7 before jumping up to the anticipated +11 of the D♭7 chord. We then continue up chromatically in quarter notes (similar to the *a* section) to the 5th of the D♭7 and then the anticipated +11 of the E♭ chord, which is tied over into **B3**.

Use Being Lazy to Your Advantage

When I was 18, I took a lesson with Manny Albam. Manny had just released a fantastic record entitled *The Soul of the City*, where nearly every track was based on the same motif. When I told him how much I liked that, he told me that he was lazy—creating new material was too much trouble and too time-consuming. Although there is a shred of truth to this, Manny was being a bit facetious. As I was starting to learn, great music comes from developing a small amount of material in the service of telling a compelling story.

The point of this is: My MO is first to see if I can repeat something. If that doesn't work, I look for previous material that I can develop. My absolute last resort is to create something new. Once I am past the exposition (head, melody chorus), even that last resort is not an option. It's too late. So, for instance in this chart, I allow no new material after letter **D**. Being particularly lazy, I don't do anything new after **B8**, and really, all of letter **B** is derived from the intro and **A**.

Repetition

With this in mind, look at **B3**. It's a copy and paste of bar **7** of the intro. It's the same E♭ chord and melody. The only difference is the orchestration. There are three great advantages of repetition:

- The listener is familiar with the material—less new stuff to figure out.
- The players are familiar with the material—less new stuff to figure out.
- You get a better performance.

Repetition gives a piece character. If every time you see me, I sport a moustache, you think, "He's the guy with the moustache," but if one day I have a moustache, and another day I don't, you might not even recognize me.

Half-steps in the Scale

Since we are committed to half-steps in this chart, it might be useful to know where the natural minor 2nds fall in the major scale. Just in case you've forgotten, they are between steps 3 and 4 (*mi fa*) and 7 and 8 (*ti do*). In **B4** we ascend the E♭ major scale starting on *la*, and progress up to *do*. Lo and behold, in this little diatonic run, we find our ascending chromatic motif (*ti do*) followed by an unimportant G and then a dramatic jump up to D (*ti*). We expect *ti* to resolve upward chromatically to *do* (E♭), but here's the big surprise: We instead fall down a minor 3rd to B♮. Where the heck did that come from? Any guesses?

This is sneaky. B♮ is the +11 of F9. Remember the A♮ (+11 of E♭) on the downbeat of **B3**? The A is followed by a C a minor 3rd above. Now, when we hear this B♮ following the D, we recognize it as the retrograde of the A and C, but transposed up a step. This makes sense melodically, but also, the F9 chord is a whole step higher than the E♭ chord. It sounds fresh, but at the same time it's kinda like we've heard it before, though we really haven't.

The Climax

Every song has a climax. At least all the successful ones do. And every arrangement has a climax. The climax in the exposition of this piece is **B5-6**. For that reason, I'm going to do some special things to draw attention to these two bars. We already have the dramatic jump up to the D and the crazy +11 (B♮) on the F9. The F9, in itself, is attention grabbing because it contains an A♮, which in the context of this diatonic bridge is a somewhat startling example of chromaticism. But that's not enough. I've gotta make sure everyone knows this is the climax, so I'm going to change the texture from the lean octave unison to a fat 13th chord in Drop 2, 4-part harmony. The bari has the red-hot A♮ on the bottom of the voicing, which adds a little spice.

Adding Counterpoint

While the four horns are holding out this colorful chord, the trombone plays a counter-line that combines the eighth notes of **B** with the descending chromatic quarter notes of **A**. The bottom three horns finish the bar with a 2-eighth-note send-off (chromatic Em7 Fm7) to the return of the trumpet/alto unison of the sixth bar of the intro (this time up an octave). Instead of resolving up to the G on the downbeat of **B8**, they slide down a half-step (we've seen this before) and then arpeggiate down an Fm triad (9, 7, 5 of B♭7) before sliding down another half-step to E♮ (♭5 of B♭7), with the other three horns filling out the root, 7th, and 3rd of the chord beneath them. To add to the drama, the rhythm section breaks for 6 beats starting in measure **B7** and rejoins the horns on the B♭7-5. I know this is a lot to grasp, but wait; there's more.

Schenker Rears His Ugly Head

When I was an undergrad Theory/Composition major, I had to read and write a critique of about 50 leading classical theory books—not exactly what I wanted to be doing at that time. One of the favorite musical theorists back then was Heinrich Schenker. Although he had been dead for 30 years, music schools were big on his methods of analysis at that time. To be honest, I don't remember much about it, except for one thing that has really stuck with me.

When you analyze a melody, you can identify and eliminate the unimportant notes and look at the shape of the underlying melody that remains. In many cases it will be either an ascending or descending line (chromatic, diatonic, or a combination). Let's take a look at the melody line of **B1-6**:

I've written the melody on the top line, and on the bottom stave I've got two sets of basic pitches from that line. I know this looks nuts, but these kinds of pitch

Example 8-2 Melody line at B1-6

sequences are key to the serialization of my melodies. I'm also careful about the serialization of the auxiliary pitches that I choose. Chuck Israels told me that he chooses the rhythm, then the shape of the line and finally the pitches. I'm not sure if I do that. It's pretty simultaneous with me, as if I'm improvising. This isn't surprising, since I want everything I write to sound as if it were improvised, only with more structure than most improvisers can achieve on the fly.

The Return of the *a* Section

Letter **C** (see *Score* p. 4/p. 109) is a repeat of **A** for 7 bars. I needed to change the last bar in order to set up the Gm11 at the top of letter **D**. Following the *ii V* patterns leading up to it, I chose Am7 D7 to take us to Gm11. The trumpet melody arpeggiates down an Em triad over the Am7 and then lands on the G#, which is the +11 of D7. It's also a half-step higher than the G we just heard on the Am7—an ascending half-step. I voiced the Am7 as an Am9 in 4-part close position with the bari on the root, then the 11th, then the root before jumping down to the low D root of the D7, which is also voiced in close position for the top four instruments.

The +11 melody replaces the chord tone just below it (F#, the 3rd). This is a bit unusual, but I like the major 7th interval between the A (5th) and the G#. The alto moves from D# (enharmonic ♭9) to E♮ (the 9th). The dissonance between the bari and alto is nice and juicy, so I thought I'd milk it a bit and have the alto resolve up to the E to draw attention.

The Return of the Intro

Letter **D** (see *Score* p. 5/p. 110) is identical to the intro, minus the initial pickup. The usage of the intro in this spot serves as an interlude, or you could think of it as an intro to the solo section of the piece.

[It's time to listen to the exposition of the piece. There will be no new material from this point on. Are we clear on the form? Are we ready to hear the players improvise on the form? Is the melody singable? Memorable? Does the arrangement fit the melody and flesh out its character? Is everyone's part idiomatic? Does it capture the hard bop aesthetic that I was going after?]

Solo Section

The solo section (Letters **E** through **H**, see *Score* pp. 6-9/pp. 111-114) has repeat signs around it. I'm leaving the order of the soloists and the number of choruses up to the discretion of whatever band will play this chart. The solo form is *aba intro*. There are backgrounds for the tenor solo in the *a* sections only. The other two sections have no backgrounds. It's quite common to alternate sections with written horn backgrounds with section of piano comping. We as listeners appreciate the space.

Backgrounds at E and G

These two sections are identical with the exception of the final bar of each, which due to different chord changes necessitated a slight alteration of pitches but the same rhythm.

Keep it Simple and Spare

The purpose of background figures is to make the soloist sound good. We don't them to be overpowered. Since this piece is dedicated to Horace Silver, it's in keeping for the written backgrounds to be like his piano comping. At the same time, I want to keep developing my motifs under the soloist. This keeps the soloist on track and gives the piece forward motion, pushing to the shout chorus.

Unison/Harmonized

The 3-note figure I chose to use for the background consists of two eighth notes in octave unison and a syncopated long note in Drop 2. The three melody notes arpeggiate up a diminished triad. The first two notes form a minor 3rd interval, just like the minor triads we used in the head. But then, instead of a major 3rd to complete a minor triad, the third note is also a minor 3rd higher, giving us a slight alteration of our motif. This lowered note creates a +5 on the dominant 7ths, which in conjunction with the other notes in the chord gives us dominant 7+9+5. This chord quality is very much in keeping with the altered dominant voicings in the head.

The Element of Surprise

Since the chord progression at **E** sequences, I'm going to keep the same rhythm for each bar and just move the horns down a half-step each time. **E4** departs from the pattern, so I have the horns rest. **E5-7** goes back to the previous pattern but starting a half-step below **E1**. **E8** breaks the pattern harmonically, so I shortened the figure. It's now just two eighth notes, but both are harmonized.

In the B♭m7-5 I substituted the 11th for the minor 3rd and then resolved to an E♭7+9. Notice that these last two voicings each have a root on the bottom. This adds more of a feeling of finality. **G8** also uses just two harmonized eighth notes, but this time it's Am7 in open position with the root on the bottom moving to a D7+11 in Drop 2. The fun element here is that the top part (trumpet) ascends by half-step (our chromatic motif).

[Let's listen to the solo section of the piece (**E-H**). How do we feel when the background comes in? Is it welcome? What is the effect eight bars later, when the rhythm section takes over the comping? And then how do we feel about the return of the background? Is the background too busy? Does it keep us in the spirit of the piece and move the development forward?]

The Shout Chorus

The shout chorus (see *Score* p. 10/p. 115) builds on the background figure from **E** and **G**. The piano plays a 3-note pickup to set it up. The first two notes are an ascending minor 3rd leading to a chord with the top note being a perfect 4th higher. This differs from the background figure in four ways:

- The interval for the third note is expanded from a minor 3rd to a perfect 4th.
- The third note is short, rather than long.
- The figure starts on the *and*-of-3 rather than the *and*-of-1.
- Because of the rhythmic displacement, the harmonized third note aligns with a m9 chord, rather than a dominant chord.

Back to Sequencing

As in the previous *a* sections, I'm going to create a 1-bar figure and sequence it through the chord progression (see *Score* p. 10/p. 115). The sequence gets broken in **I4** and **I8**. Actually, the sequence begins in the piano on the eighth note before **I** with the Am9. The piano then alternates dominant 7+9+5 with minor 9th chords. The pattern is long/short with each note starting on the *and*-of-2 and then the *and-of-4*. Both are voiced in Drop 2 with an added root on the bottom. The top notes of each chord form a descending chromatic scale (the inversion of our original motif). Each piano note is answered by the unison horns a beat later with their long eighth note and short quarter—first up a minor 3rd and then up a minor 2nd (our original motif).

Switching Roles

This overlapping call-and-response is a bit dizzying. When the pattern is broken in **I4**, the horns go into 5-part harmony on the E♭maj9, but only for a beat. Immediately, the trumpet and alto go back to the unison offbeat pattern for two notes but then return to join the other horns for the long/short voicings. In **A4** there are passing chords to walk up from the E♭ chord to the Abm7 in **A5**. In **I4** the rhythm section stays on the E♭ for the entire bar and then resolves down a 5th to A♭m7 in **I5**. The three harmonized chords in the horns are E♭maj9, up a half-step (our motif) E7+9, and E♭maj7. The trumpet and alto switch back and forth from unison to harmonized in this bar. This change of texture happens throughout the entire piece, becoming part of its character.

Back to the Sequence

I5-7 is identical to **I1-3** except transposed down a minor 2nd. All this repeated material gives the chart continuity and enables the listener to understand some complex relationships. The more we repeat, the more they can grasp. The pattern is broken the eighth note before **I8**. It looks like we are going to do a minor *ii V* into the bridge in A♭ major, but at the last second, I throw in a *IV* chord in A♭—making a plagal (churchy) cadence. What prompted that was the G in the melody. It becomes the intriguing +11 of the D♭7 rather than the staid major 3rd of a repeated E♭7.

Repeating the E♭7 chord feels static to me, so I opted for the unusual *V7 IV7* approach to the A♭ I say "unusual," but we know this progression from the blues. In traditional blues it often happens in bars **9-12** (a bar of *V*, a bar of *IV*, and two bars of *I*). I kept the horns in unison for the first two beats of **I8** since they are arpeggiating quickly. Plus, alternating unison and harmonized textures is a big part of the fabric of this chart. Note the chromatically descending melodic line in the basic pitches of **I8** (D♭, C, C♭, B♭).

Further Development

Letter **J** (see *Score* p. 11/p. 116) is the *b* section of the form. **J1-3** develops the material in **I4**: rhythmic voicings with independent trumpet/alto unison eighth note ascending minor 2nds. To avoid static harmonies in **J1** and **J3**, I used a dominant 7th chord a half-step higher. In **J1** the voicings are A♭maj7, A9, A♭6. In **J3** it's E♭maj9 and E7+9. The horns don't return to the E♭ chord, but the trumpet/alto unison states an E♭ on beat 4 and the rhythm section stays on E♭ for the entire measure (ignoring the E7 altogether). When passing chords are fleeting in the horns, it's often wise not to inform the rhythm section about them. If they catch every passing chord, it can disrupt their flow and impede the swing.

How far can we go with our chromatic motif?

The answer is: pretty damn far. **J4** is a descending chromatic scale in all the parts. It starts on Cm9 and descends chromatically down a tritone to G♭m7. The original chord which should occur in **J5** is F7, which should last for two measures. To accommodate my chromatic run, I substituted G♭m9, held it for a bar and then resolved to the F7 with both a +9 and a -9.

Remember the B♮ climax in B5-6?

Well, it's back in **J6**, but this time, all the horns are in unison and there are three of them.

Bringing Back the Pattern for One Last Measure

J7 returns to the pattern of **J1** with the lower three horns playing voicings and the trumpet and alto switching back and forth between harmony and unison. This time the Fm7 chord repeats rather than moving up a half-step, but finally at the end of the bar, it moves down a half-step anticipating the B♭7 of the next bar. Notice the melody combining the downward Cm arpeggio over Fm7 and the G to G♭ chromatic resolution (our inverted half-step motif).

Implied Tritone Subs

Although **J8** is a B♭7 in the rhythm section, the horns anticipate the harmony with an E9 (the tritone sub of B♭7). There is no need to inform the rhythm section of this substitution. A long time ago, I noticed that pianists frequently would employ tritone subs while the bassist stayed with the original chord change. Sometimes the bassist stays on the dominant while the pianist plays the tritone sub, and vice versa—often bassists will play a tritone sub while the harmony above it stays on the original dominant chord.

Repeating the *a* section

Letter K (see *Score* p. 12/p. 117) is a direct repeat of **I** except for the final bar (**K8**), which puts a period on the shout chorus. There is the ascending Am9 arpeggio (bar **1** of the intro transposed up a step) followed by a D7+9 chord with an added fall-off to help smooth over the transition. It's nice to cover up the seams, so that the form isn't in our face.

On beat 4 the rhythm section gives us the pickup that started the piece, and we *D.S.* back to measure **1** of the intro. We play the intro, **A, B, C**, and the first six bars of **D** before going to the Coda (see *Score* p. 13/p. 118), which is very similar to **D7**—only with a surprising final chord. The melody moves chromatically down to D♭ (the m7 of our key of E♭), but instead of harmonizing it with the typical tonic chord (in this case E♭7), I chose to make the D♭ melody the +9 of a B♭7+9+5 (the dominant of E♭).

Ending on the dominant is like an ending with a question mark? It's like the ending to a Preston Sturges romantic comedy: They all lived happily ever after... or did they? In this case, E♭7 with a D♭ on top would sound out of place. We have no such chords in the entire piece. But what chord do we have more than any other? Dominant 7+9+5. Case closed.

One Last Thing

I've said this many times, but at least 90% of the things I've talked about in this analysis were unknown to my conscious mind while I wrote this chart. I only discovered them while writing the book years later. While I was composing and arranging, I was just imagining what would be a piece I would enjoy playing and listening to.

[Let's first listen to the shout chorus (letters **I-K**). Do we feel satisfied that we have developed our initial material sufficiently? Is the climax at **J5-6** satisfying?

Now let's listen to the entire piece. Does it all hang together? Does it feel inevitable when each section occurs? Is there sufficient surprise throughout, or does all the repetition make this piece sound predictable? Does everyone get a part that is fun to play? After Duke Ellington would rehearse a new Billy Strayhorn chart, Billy would walk around the room and ask the individual players if they liked their part.]

9. Silver's Standard
   Octet Arrangement

As with my other two homages to Horace Silver, I didn't have anyone in mind when I started composing this tune. In this case, I was sitting at the piano and played the first three notes voiced out with my two hands. That's all I needed. The rest just spilled out easily in less than an hour. At that time, I was playing Tuesday nights at Birdland with my big band, so I scored this tune for us to play. As I was arranging it, I kept thinking that it might be more appropriate for an octet. Since I didn't have an octet to play such a chart, I put that idea on hold for a decade, until I started writing **Creative Jazz Composing and Arranging III: Writing for Small Groups.**

The two main reasons for including **Silver's Standard** in this book are the 7-bar *a* sections and the stepwise diatonic chord progression in **A5-7**. Although these two quirky aspects define most of the character of this piece, there are many more pertinent issues in the rest of the piece that aren't addressed in the other pieces included in this volume.

Hard Bop

Like *The Silver Bullet*, the genre is hard bop. When I was growing up in New York in the 1950's and early '60s, hard bop was the prevailing style of jazz. I was hearing new tunes nightly, many of which have become jazz standards. Besides Horace Silver, there was Art Blakey and the Jazz Messengers, Blakey alumni Freddie Hubbard and Wayne Shorter, The Jazztet (with Benny Golson, Art Farmer, and Curtis Fuller), Lee Morgan, Cannonball Adderley, and so many other groups. They added a bit of Gospel influence to bebop along with more simplified and tuneful melodies.

Naming Tunes

The title, **Silver's Standard**, refers obliquely to America's currency in silver coins and paper backed in silver as well as both the benchmark of quality that Horace set throughout his career and how so many of his tunes became jazz standards that we are still playing more than a half century later. I take care in naming my tunes. I want the title to be catchy and roll off the tongue, which accounts for the alliteration in this title. But also, I want to give the listener a clue or two about how to begin to understand the piece. Silver himself often took a similar approach to naming his own tunes.

Form

Silver's Standard is written in the typical *aaba* song form with one glaring eccentricity: whereas *aaba* songs almost always are written in 8-bar phrases, the *a* sections in this tune are all seven measures long. I didn't set out to write a 7-bar phrase. The tune just went there, and I didn't want to stop it. I tested it to see if it felt natural. I'm not a fan of "science projects." I don't like music to be weird for the sake of trying to be different. After playing through the tune a few times, I decided that there was a natural flow. Bar **A4** serves as both the fourth bar of the first phrase and the first bar of the second phrase. Adding another measure to conform to a 4-square structure would be superfluous and impede the forward motion.

The form of the arrangement (see *Score* pp. 1-7/pp. 132-138) is:
- Head: *aaba*
- Solo Choruses: *aaba* repeated for extra choruses and/or different soloists
- Shout half chorus: *aa*
- Recapitulation: *ba* with a fermata

Introduction or No Introduction?

There is no introduction. Very often tunes that begin with a break or stop time figure (like this one) can be more striking if there is no preparation. Also, there are no solo backgrounds and no coda. This piece didn't seem to warrant them. My goal in writing music isn't to write as much as possible but just what is needed. "Less is more."

Head

(See *Score* p. 1/p. 132.) Sometimes when I start composing a new piece, I don't know what key it's in. I must wait until it cadences before I determine the key signature. Such was the case with **Silver's Standard**. The melodic opening interval of an ascending perfect 4th (G to C) might suggest *sol do* in C or C minor. I won't know for sure until the harmony settles on the E♭6 chord on the third beat of **A7**.

Once I completed the melody and harmonization of letter **A**, I was able to assign the key signature of three flats, which was determined by the final cadence in E♭ major and the diatonic bass line starting on the second beat of **A4**.

Using Key Signatures

Whenever possible, I use key signatures. Almost all my music is tonal. The key centers change, but they usually cadence in a major or minor key or a mode. Key signatures help the players understand their parts. If you know where *do* is, you have a pretty good shot at hearing the other pitches in relationship to the key. If there is no key signature, I am forced to rely solely on the intervals between the pitches, since I don't have perfect pitch. The bridges of tunes normally modulate, so I'm not concerned with what key they are in, since they will ultimately return to the *a* section.

SILVER'S STANDARD – OCTET ARRANGEMENT

The Motif

The first three notes at **A** (including the pickup) make up the motif that generates the rest of the piece. Melodically, it's an ascending 4th followed by a descending minor 2nd. This 3-note figure is then sequenced twice, continuing the descending minor 2nds. The G quarter note pickup is repeated in **A1** and then lowered a whole step in **A2** to replicate the ascending minor 3rd interval from the previous bar. When the opening G is reached in the chromatically descending line (on the *and*-of-2 in **A3**), it drops a perfect 5th to C (this perfect 5th is an inversion of the opening ascending perfect 4th). The ascending minor 3rd from C to E♭ settles on the tonic (E♭) for an entire measure.

Sequencing

The simplest development technique is repetition. Sequences repeat the rhythm but transpose the pitches to a different key or different step of the scale. **A1-3** is a combination of a diatonic and chromatic sequence—a 1-bar figure repeated twice, with each repeat a whole step lower than the previous bar. Sometimes it's satisfying to repeat sequences verbatim, and sometimes it feels right to make slight adjustments that tie into the motif and/or help establish the key. **A1-3** is the later.

The Ascending Minor 3rd Motif

The G in **A2** moving to the B♭ in **A3** introduces the ascending minor 3rd interval, which will recur a measure later (F to A♭) as well as in the next measure C to E♭. More minor 3rds occur in **A4** and **6**, **B3-4** and **7-8**). They also appear in the inside parts, most notably ascending and descending in the bari in **A1-2**.

The Diatonic Context

Although there are two melodic chromatic pitches and highly chromatic harmony, these first four bars are basically in E♭ major. The melodic C♭ and A♮ serve to connect diatonic notes in a descending E♭ major scale. The D♭7-5 chord in **A3** functions as a *bVII7* in E♭. We expect it to resolve to the tonic E♭ chord. The melody confirms our E♭ major suspicions, but the harmony substitutes the *#ivm7-5* for the tonic (Am7-5 in place of E♭). This tritone-related chord is a common tonic substitute used in the reharmonization of many standard songs like the opening of Harold Arlen's *Somewhere Over The Rainbow* and *I Should Care*.

Answering the High Instruments with the Low Instruments

The E♭ whole note is answered in the bass clef with an eighth note line, which begins with an ascending minor 3rd (*mi sol* in E♭) before returning to the starting G and ascending to the E♭ scale with an A♮ chromatic lower neighbor alteration—which implies E♭ Lydian (A being the raised 4). The line continues up to C *(la)* and then D *(ti)*, which is displaced by an octave. Octave displacement is a great technique for making your music more angular.

Continuing the Line in the Top Instruments

Back in the treble instruments, the line continues up the scale to the tonic (E♭). The chromatic turn (F♭) is employed rather than the diatonic F♮, so that when the F♮ appears later in the bar, it will sound fresh.

E♭ Scale with Chromatics

Dipping back down to C, we begin a scalewise climb to the dominant (B♭) with the D♭ chromatic alteration implying E♭7 (tonic with a ♭7, as in the blues) and employing the half-step between F and G. Notice that the A♮, D♭, and F# are the three blue notes in the key of E♭. After reaching the peak B♭, we drop down a minor 3rd to G, which will repeat as the pickup to the repeat of letter **A**. The proliferation of minor 3rds and minor 2nds is starting to look (and sound) suspicious.

Modulating for the Bridge

The melody of the bridge at **B** (see *Score* p. 2/p. 133) begins in F minor. The descending tritone in **B2** is both startling and integral to the piece. The G♭ (a blue note in the key of E♭, by the way) is the ♭5 on the C7 but also implies the root of the tritone-related G♭7, which will then resolve down a half-step to Fm. The abundance of Fs and A♭'s in **B3-4** reprises our ascending minor 3rd motif.

One Good Turn Deserves Another

The 16th note turn refers to the chromatic turn in **A5**. The chromatic upper neighbor is now "corrected" to the diatonic B♭, which foreshadows the B♭s in the following phrase, where B♭ becomes the dominant of our old friend E♭ major.

The 2-bar Sequential Figure on the Bridge

B5-6 is a sequence of **B1-2**. This 2-bar sequential figure has a nice relationship to the 1-bar sequential figure in **A1-3**. The ascending minor 3rd motif returns with a vengeance in **B7-8**. **B8** is a sequence of **B7** (*ii V* patterns down a whole step). Letter **C** is a copy and paste of **A**. This completes the melody for the *aaba* head.

[There's a lot going on here melodically. Let's take a moment and listen to **A** through **C**. Does it hang together? Is the bridge different enough from the *a* section? Do we feel relieved at the return of *a* at letter **C**?

Conventional songwriting says that the highest note should appear 2/3 to 3/4 of the way through the tune. Here both the *a* section and bridge start with the highest note. Is that a problem? I'm not big on rules and formulas. There are many successful tunes that defy the rules.

Lastly, is this melody catchy? Do you sing it easily? Does it stick with you?]

Harmonizing the Head

Although the straightforward melody of this tune has a certain amount of charm, the harmonies are far more complex. The dichotomy of simple and complex make this tune easy to understand on one level (melodically) and challenging to follow on another (harmonically).

Don't fix it if it ain't broke.

My first instinct in developing material is to repeat. If that is too predictable, then I need to think of something else. Sequences are the closest things to outright repetition. As the melody repeats starting on a different pitch, so can the harmonies. This is the formula for **A1-3**: **A2** is a whole step below **A1**, and **A3** is a whole step below **A2**.

Doubling the Melody

I wanted to stick to 4-part voicings in the horns. Adding octave doublings or extra pitches didn't feel right to me—it would be a loss of intimacy. I was hearing four parts, but there were five horns staring me in the face. My solution was to double the alto sax with the trumpet on the top notes of the chords. This will give the ensemble more of a homogeneous blend and preclude any individual personality. Unisons must be played straight to be in tune and blend. I'll keep this doubling throughout the head.

Moving the Motif from the Top to the Bottom

There's a little trick in the voicings. The bari has the root of the F#m7-5 but then jumps up a minor 3rd (oops! There is that pesky motif—this time it's moved from the top part to the bari) to be the 3rd of the F9+11 chord. The other voices move down when they resolve from the m7-5 to the dominant, creating contrary motion. The reason for all this is that the F# root on the half-diminished is important in establishing the tritone between the root and the ♭5 in the melody. On the F7 chord, I wanted to create the tritone between the b7 (E♭) and the 3rd (A). The bassist has the F covered. The melody that the bari plays was the selling point for me.

Signaling an Upcoming Change

Notice the subtle change on the D♭7-5 in **A3**. I disrupted the repetition (it was great once, but was becoming predictable, and besides I want to announce that a new texture is coming) and move everyone down chromatically except for the tenor, who repeats his F. This also makes for an interesting part for the tenor. His repeated pitches set him off from all the other horns and create oblique motion.

CJCA III: WRITING FOR SMALL GROUPS

SILVER'S STANDARD

David Berger

Example 9-1 *Silver's Standard* octet score, page 1

SILVER'S STANDARD – OCTET ARRANGEMENT

Example 9-1 *Silver's Standard* octet score, page 2

CJCA III: WRITING FOR SMALL GROUPS

Example 9-1 *Silver's Standard* octet score, page 3

SILVER'S STANDARD – OCTET ARRANGEMENT

Example 9-1 Silver's Standard octet score, page 4

CJCA III: WRITING FOR SMALL GROUPS

Example 9-1 Silver's Standard octet score, page 5

SILVER'S STANDARD – OCTET ARRANGEMENT

Example 9-1 Silver's Standard octet score, page 6

CJCA III: WRITING FOR SMALL GROUPS

Silver's Standard

Example 9-1 Silver's Standard *octet score, page 7*

SILVER'S STANDARD – OCTET ARRANGEMENT

Example 9-1 *Silver's Standard* octet score, page 8

CJCA III: WRITING FOR SMALL GROUPS

Example 9-1 Silver's Standard octet score, page 9

Pickup Unisons

I used octave unisons for all the pickups. I could have harmonized them, but that would have taken away some of the surprise on the half-diminished voicings. We notice changes in texture. Use them to your advantage.

Switching to Unison Line Over 3-Part Harmony

The bottom instruments play a unison answer in **A4**, with the rhythm section providing *ii V I* in Gm. Gm is the chord built on the third step of E♭ and is closely related since both keys contain mostly the same pitches (the only different ones are A♮ and F#, which are blue notes in E♭).

Changing the Harmonic Rhythm

The unison line is then passed to the trumpet/alto unison in **A5-7**, while the bass and bari walk down an E♭ scale and the tenor and trombone flesh out passing harmonies. The harmonic rhythm has switched from two beats per chord to a chord on every beat. This gives the illusion that the music is moving at a faster tempo. Most of these chords are diatonic. The only accidentals are D♭ (♭7 blue note) and B♮.

Open Harmony

Each chord is constructed in 4-part open harmony with the unison line being the top voice of the harmonies. The parallel structures in the bottom three parts provide continuity and forward motion and opposition to the unison line in the trumpet and alto.

Break on the Bridge

The 2-bar break at the start of the bridge provides drama but it also is a development of the stop time of **A1-3**. The lack of accompanying harmony adds to the break effect.

Thumb Line

When the tenor and bari enter with their 5, #5, 6, 7 thumb line on the Fm chord, it's all the more effective coming out of the starkness of the preceding 2-bar break. The ascending chromatic thumb line is a retrograde version of **A1-2** with smoothed out rhythm. When disguised *a* material is used in other sections of the piece, it's unifying without being overt.

Writing for Bari

In a small group like this, the bari can function as an inside part (leaving the roots to the bassist) or play roots in the low register, which can make the band sound much bigger than its numbers. **B5** (see *Score* p. 2/p. 133) starts with the bari on the 3rd of the D7+9 with the trombone and tenor above on the 7th and +9. The trumpet/alto unison moves from the +5 to the natural 5 (retrograde of the thumb line in **B3**).

Spread Chords (Chorale Voicings)

B6-8 has the bari on low roots in open voicings. The Gm7-5 F#7-5 is reminiscent of the chromatic changes in **A1-3**, but it is in a completely different context on the bridge. Although the B♭7 in **B5** signals the return to the key of E♭ on the repeat of the *a* section, the chromatic chords that follow take a circuitous route. Surprisingly, it gets us there. The final D♭m7-5 (enharmonically respelled C#m7-5) is built a perfect 5th above the F#m7-5 at **C** and has the same chord quality (half-diminished).

Melody/Accompaniment Contrast

A concept I picked up from Ellington and Strayhorn is to differentiate between a solo or unison line and the supporting pads both rhythmically and melodically. Avoid melody notes in the supporting harmonies. Occasionally, we might deviate with a moment of octave doubling. This happens with the 3rd on the E7 chord in measure **B7**. It's best to keep the doubling to a minimum.

[Let's listen to the head (**A** through **C**). Do the harmonies and orchestration bring out the character of the melody, or do they obscure it? Are they surprising while feeling inevitable, or does this come across as too weird? At the end of letter **C**, do you feel like launching into a solo? Does the head inspire you to improvise?]

Solo Choruses

Because the head was so complex, I wanted to keep the solo choruses (see *Score* pp. 4-7/pp. 135-138) simple, so I wrote no horn backgrounds. When considering what chord changes to use for the blowing, sometimes the chords from the head are fun to blow on, and sometimes they can be a bit too complicated. I want the soloists to feel comfortable, so I give them changes that I would feel comfortable blowing on.

Getting Rid of Clutter

In this case, the opening four bars are fun for any bebop player. The Gm and A7 in the fifth bar are fine. We don't need the clutter of the C#m7-5. It was fine to support the melody of the head, but too confining to improvise over. The same is true for bars **6** and **7**. A chord change on every beat is too much. How about if instead of speeding up the harmonic rhythm, we slow it down to one bar per change? The basic chords in measures **A6-7** are Dm7-5 to G7, so let's just go with that.

7-bar Phrases

The big decision is whether to improvise on 7-bar phrases or smooth it out to a more regular eight. I decided to stay with seven, since it feels comfortable and is unique to this tune. If it presents a problem for the players, I'd be amenable to changing it.

Making the Bridge a Soft Place to Land

A similar harmonic issue occurs on the bridge. The first four bars are fine. Rather than run the obstacle course in bars **B5-6**, I decided to stick with the B♭7 for two bars. This makes the first six bars of the bridge a soft place to land. I decided to keep the last two bars of the bridge, even with the one beat of C#m7-5, since D7 moving to F#m7-5 doesn't feel like a resolution. F#m7-5 is the chord built on the 3rd of D7. Letter **G** (see *Score* p 7/p. 138) is the same as **D**.

Repeats Within Repeats

If you are wondering why I wrote out the *a* section of this chorus twice instead of putting a repeat around eight bars, it's because the entire chorus (**D-G**) repeats, and it would be very confusing (and not kosher!) to write repeats within a repeat.

[Listen to the solo section. Does it feel comfortable for the soloists and rhythm section? It's challenging but not intimidating. I want it to be fun. If it's fun for the players, it should be fun for the listeners as well.

I rely on the players to create the dynamics based on where the soloists and rhythm section are going. I can't know that ahead of time since they will be improvising. With pieces that we play often, players find things that work, and sometimes they get memorialized. I tend to not want to write those things into the arrangement, and instead, leave it up to the players to remember the routine.

All the music in this book was rehearsed and recorded in one 4-hour session, so there was no time for the music to develop as it might in a steady club gig or on tour. My musicians are seasoned pros and make the music happen quickly, but our experience over many years is that the music gets better over time. There is no substitute for repeated performances.]

Shout Chorus

Rather than a traditional shout or sock chorus, this piece seemed to want to get smaller at this juncture. Of the thousands of charts I've written, this shout chorus stays the closest to the material in the head. The change in groove is the main piece of development. The form, pitches, harmonies, orchestration, and dynamics stay close to home.

Marches

New Orleans jazz evolved out of American marches mixed with the blues. I first played the stock arrangement of *St. Louis Blues March* as a teen in the 1960s. When I heard the Glenn Miller record, I put it in context with Sousa's *Entry Of The Gladiators*, and all the other traditional marches that were so popular in the early 1900s, and were still a mainstay of high school concert bands.

Jazz Marches

Around the same time, The Jazztet recorded Benny Golson's *Blues March*, which became an immediate jazz standard, translating the march into the hard bop genre. Shortly afterwards, I became a Monday night regular at the Village Vanguard and was thrilled by Thad Jones' chart of his brother Hank's *A-That's Freedom*. Then I heard Duke Pearson's quintet recording of *Gaslight* with its march shout chorus, and Les Brown's recording of Prokofiev's March from the opera *The Love for Three Oranges*. With all these sounds floating around in my head, it now seems odd to me that I've hardly ever explored the jazz march groove in my own compositions and arrangements.

Change the Rhythm and Keep Everything Else

As in *Gaslight,* the march groove appears only for a short segment at the beginning of the shout chorus. The same melody, harmony, orchestration, and dynamics of **A1-2** prevail in **H1-2** (see *Score* p. 8/p. 139). The rhythm is changed slightly to conform with the drums. Three staccato quarters replace the long/short syncopation. This new stiff rhythm conveys the bellicose nature of marches and leaves it up to the drummer to supply just a pinch of swing feel and looseness to the groove.

Introducing Independence and Syncopation

H3-4 gently diverges from the lockstep coordination of the previous two bars. The first two beats are quarter notes, but the trumpet/alto unison melody is alone on beat 2. They stay in unison for the next two notes while joined by the tenor in contrary motion a 3rd below.

Alto Independence

For the only time so far in the chart, the alto splits off from the trumpet for a measure starting with the Am9-5 on the *and*-of-4 in **H3**. He continues to express his independence, not only pitchwise but also rhythmically for all of **H4**, turning the melody of **H3** around underneath the trumpet lead. The alto's line is basically a descending chromatic scale with a ghosted G eighth note inserted. His pitches tease us with tensions on the chords. On the Am7-5 he plays 9, 7, and -9. On the D7-9 he plays 5 and ♭5 (ending a tritone below the trumpet lead on the D).

Keeping the Form

As in **A4-7**, the trumpet/alto unison eighth note line is pitted against the descending diatonic walking bass line in the bass and bari as we return to the swing feel. The tenor and trombone flesh out the harmonies, taking into account the unison melody notes above them.

Sameness and Difference

We need a certain amount of difference in the shout chorus to feel the music building and to surprise us. But, at the same time, we need to retain enough elements of the exposition for continuity. We would feel cheated if there were no relationship to the previous motifs. This entire 7-bar section is constructed of minor 3rds, descending chromatics, and tritones. Even the inner voices above the walking bass contain almost entirely melodic tritones, 2nds, and 3rds. The icing on the cake is the 16th note turn in **H6**—a bar later than its predecessor in **A5**. These seven measures are interesting enough to bear repetition.

Recapitulation

Rather that finish the chorus form in the shout, it feels like it's time to return to the bridge of the head and take it out by repeating letters **B** and **C**. This is typical, especially in medium or slow tempi. Uptempo numbers are more likely to demand a full shout chorus rather than splitting the chorus with the recap.

Returning Home, and Nothing's Changed, Except Our Point of View

Most recaps use the material of the head verbatim. Now that we've experienced our adventure of development, we hear the head again, but with more understanding. Our next problem is how to end this piece.

Do We Need a Coda?

If we can arrive at a conclusion without adding extra material, all the better. As I mentioned, I'm a firm believer in "less is more."

Ending on the Tonic

When I was in high school, I asked my band director if every piece should end on the tonic. Being an accomplished, albeit conventional, arranger, he answered in the affirmative. That might have been true for the classics, but I was intent in disproving his rule. Sure enough, exceptions were all around me—especially in the current jazz records and performances at that time (mid-'60s). Some pieces just want to leave the listener with a question mark or an unsettling feeling.

Alternate Final Chords

Although the great majority of jazz arrangements end on the tonic, it's become a cliché to end on the ♭*II* or ♭*VII7*. I've even ended on the *V*. Basically, if you hold a chord long enough, it will start to feel like the tonic. My process is to write a strong melody that is in keeping with the central motif. Then I write a bass line that makes the melody sound good and feels satisfying. This usually means that the bass will resolve in a strong functional pattern like the circle of 5ths or chromatically up or down.

Melodic Tension

I often like the final melody note to be a tension of the chord (9, 11, 13 or alterations). Such is the case in **Silver's Standard**. The trumpet melody is the same on the final chord as it was in **A6**. What has changed is that, instead of descending diatonically to B♭6, the bass descends chromatically to B. The G in the trumpet suggested a B7+5 chord. Since the bari has been descending in unison with the bass roots, I gave the tenor and trombone the 3rd and 7th. I could continue to couple the alto in unison with the trumpet, but it would help to signal the final cadence if he jumped down to a +9.

Tying Up Loose Ends

This figure ties up the loose end of the alto's independence in **H3-4**. If something happens once in a piece, we crave for it to come back—if not verbatim, then in some form. And so, we conclude a piece in E♭ major on a B7+9+5 chord (altered shoulder chord). I can't think that I've ever done that before. I didn't *think* to do it. Everything just seemed to want to go there.

[Let's listen to the entire track. My questions are:

- Is there enough surprise to keep us interested?
- Does the form of the 7-bar *a* section feel natural or contrived?
- Is there enough excitement? Is it okay that the melody climaxes on the first bar and the trumpet never plays above the staff?
- Is the change in dynamics in the solo section sufficient to give the piece shape, since the written sections are all at *mf*?
- The ending is intended to be unsettling. Did I go too far?]

10. In A Persian Market Octet Score

Here's another octet chart that is quite different from the previous two in a number of ways. I wrote it specifically for the purpose of this book, in order to present a number of topics that I hadn't covered previously.

The tune itself is from what we used to call "light classical," an orientalist piece evocative of the Middle East. I was attracted to the multi-theme *ABA* structure: the herky-jerky Arabic groove of the *A* theme and the contrasting smooth romantic setting of the *B* theme. I added a 5/4 pseudo-Arabic intro/outro, a swing solo section, and a rhumba shout chorus, making the form Intro, *A*, *B*, Solos, Shout, *A*, Intro. Since the shout is based on the *B* (rhumba theme), the overall effect is like a rondo: Intro, *ABCBA*, Intro. No one groove stays for too long, and there is sufficient variety in the melodic and harmonic material to keep us interested and surprised. The Arabic and rhumba sections use even eighth notes, while the interior solo section is played with swing eighths. The effect of going into swing is one of relaxation and freedom from the rigidity of the even Arabic and rhumba grooves.

Just to be clear, I'm not concerned about the authenticity of influences outside of jazz. My only criteria is: does it sound good to me? Outside influences are appropriated for added color and contrast. This is to say that in no way is this authentic Iranian music, nor is it meant to be. I only wanted to create a Middle Eastern flavor, as did Albert Ketèlbey, the original composer.

Changing Grooves

One of the hardest things to do in jazz is to change grooves and/or tempi without sounding pretentious or artificial. Since this piece changes groove with each section, it took some care to create the seams and to get the performers to be convincing and keep a steady tempo. Changing grooves is central to this piece and will be addressed in the intro, but for now, let's examine the *A* theme, since that is where I established the motifs that will be previewed in the intro. If I remember correctly, I scored letter **A** before I wrote the intro, which is normal for me.

A Theme

This theme is quite simple. It consists of a 1-bar motif in the piccolo and piano in double octaves at **A1** (see *Score* p. 3/p. 160): three quarter notes preceded by ascending chromatic grace notes and followed by two eighth notes a tritone apart (B♭ and E) built a half-step higher than the previous quarter notes. Basically, we are dealing with minor seconds and a tritone.

Grace Notes

Although the grace notes add to the Arabic color, they are embellishments and not as important as the other notes in the measure. I'm not at all considering them in the harmony (Am).

Harmonizing the Motif

It's very clear to me that this section is in A minor. It starts on the tonic and ends in a semi-cadence (the dominant—E7). In fact, the B♭ on beat 4 of our motif signals the minor 9th of the dominant (A7-9) with the final E as the 5th of the chord. The resulting tritone between the B♭ and the E creates an exotic atmosphere, especially in conjunction with the previous A's.

What Goes Up Must Come Down

Measure **A2** (see *Score* p. 3/p. 160) inverts the motif by having the final eighth notes descend rather than ascend. They further develop the original idea by altering the intervals—descending by a major 2nd from the A and then down a minor 3rd from G to E. Notice how the A, G and E are the root, 7th and 5th of the tonic (Am). However, I'm going to stick with tonic/dominant pattern of the first bar (**A1**) and add some blues color by making the G, E the +9 and root of the dominant (E7). I've used the tritone sub of E7 (B♭7) to avoid the melody and bass unison on the E on beat 4.

Foreground Becomes Background

Since we've just heard the B♭ in the melody of the previous bar, it is not all that surprising to move the B♭ from the foreground (melody) to the background (bass line). Reversing foreground and background is a great unifying technique.

Repetition is the simplest way to develop an idea.

A3 is identical to **A1**. **A4** gives us the downbeat of **A1**, but minus the grace note, which is removed to create a short, accented downbeat. The rest of the bar is left blank until the last eighth note, which is a pickup into the next measure.

Sequencing is the next easiest developmental technique.

A5-8 is exactly the same as **A1-4** except transposed down a 4th, so that we are temporarily in the key of Em (built on the dominant note of A minor). This is very common in music previous to the 20th century—after which, American popular music more commonly used the subdominant rather than the dominant for temporary modulations. Think of any number of American standards like Billy Strayhorn's *Take The "A" Train* or Fats Waller's *Honeysuckle Rose*, where the bridge either begins on the subdominant or arrives there quickly.

Chromatic Color

A subtle touch that comes with these four bars on the modal dominant (Em) is the chromatic alteration on its dominant (the D# on the B7 chords) and then the final G# on the E7 in **A8**. The E7 is the turnaround to take us back to Am on the repeat of letter **A**.

Counterpoint in the Bass

The bass line in **A1** is the rhythmic opposite of the melody; where the melody has quarter notes, the bass has eighths, and vice versa. They fit together hand-in-glove. To preserve the Arabic flavor and simplicity, I stuck with roots and fifths in the bass making use of the lowest note on the bass (open E string) on beat four. This adds color.

A2 is identical, except for the tritone sub Bb replacing the low E adding melodic and harmonic interest. **A3** repeats **A1** verbatim—

If repeating something sounds good, that will be your strongest choice. It will add continuity and character to your music. It makes it easier for the listener to understand the form, and at the same time making it easier for the performers to play your music.

Building Breaks into the Fabric of the Piece

The drum break in **A4** sets us up to expect more breaks later... in fact, we will be disappointed if we don't get them. When they occur in **A8**, the repeat of **A4**, **A9** and finally **G4** (see *Score* p. 10/p. 167), they are most welcome. Giving the rhythm section players a chance to shine adds a dimension to octet arrangements that usually feature the horns.

Doubling the Bass and Melody Lines

Except for walking bass lines in swing charts, it's common to double the bass in other instruments. I debated whether to double it in the piano, but chose to double the bass with the piano and bass clarinet, which is more delicate than the piano. To avoid heaviness, I generally double the bass in the same octave, if possible. Remember, the bass sounds an octave below where written.

On the other hand, I chose to double the piccolo in the piano in double octaves. The piccolo sounds an octave higher than where written. The piano will give the piccolo more body.

Adding Punches on the 2nd and 3rd Time

Keeping in mind that trumpets and trombones can add fire and accents, I added them in the chords that appear on the *and*-of-four in **A1-7** as wells as on the *and*-of-one in **A4** and on beat 2 in **A8**. Since the piccolo is playing the root of the dominant (E7 or B♭7 in **A1-3** or B7 or F7 in **A5-7**), I gave the brass the 3rd and 7th of the chords.

On the *and*-of-one in **A4**, I had the clarinet join them for an F7 (the tritone sub for the dominant of the upcoming Em). Again, I kept the brass on the 3rd and 7th and gave the clarinet the F root on top. In **A8** the chord on beat 2 is the turnaround E7+9. The brass plays their usual 3rd and 7th, while the clarinet tremolos +9 to ♭5, adding a funky element to the otherwise stiff Persian market.

Adding an Element to Make the 3rd Time Interesting

It's common practice to add a new idea on the repeat of a section. I saved the clarinet precisely for this purpose. It's a fresh color and can play in the tessitura between the brass and piccolo.

Basic Contrapuntal Concepts

On the most basic level, counterpoint involves different rhythms and pitches. In letter **A**, the melody, bass and hits have all the eighth notes and quarter notes covered. I could write slower rhythms (half notes, dotted halves, whole notes, etc.) or faster rhythms (16ths, 32nds, etc.). I chose to give the 3rd time at **A** more forward motion by adding 16th notes. The clarinet is emphasizing the minor 2nd and tritone intervals in our motif in **A1**. I've connected the two with ascending and descending scales. In contrast to the tongued notes in the other horns, the clarinet line is slurred (legato). It's important that it be as seemingly opposite as possible from everything else that is going on, while developing the same material to give it cohesion.

Intro

Let's go back and look at the intro now. The purpose of most intros is to set the tempo and groove. This is often given to the piano or the entire rhythm section, and then the horns come in at letter **A** with the melody. That's kinda like what happens here, except that the groove, which is set up by the rhythm section (quarter note pulse), feels twice as slow as the groove at letter **A** (eighth note pulse). In addition, the intro has a 5/4 meter that abruptly shifts to an 8/8 feel at **A**. This change is unprepared, and as a result, packs a lot of drama.

Setting up the Motifs

To create continuity and to make the intro not only relevant but a forecaster of what the piece is about, I started with the piccolo melody of **A1-2** and gave it to the bass (doubled in the piano left hand), adding a syncopation and a ghosted low E eighth note. The syncopation necessitated an extra beat—hence the 5/4 meter. I kept the descending minor 3rd G to E in the 2nd measure but changed the pitches of beat four and five in measure **1**. As I've said before, I love when foreground becomes background. In this case the bass line background will become the piccolo foreground at **A**.

Adding Harmony

I used the bass notes as roots and built minor chords in the piano right hand, alternating between minor 7th chords (C/A, F/D, B♭/G) and minor 9th chords with no 7ths (Cm, Em). The half-steps in these minor 9th chords sets up our minor 2nd melodic motif at letter **A**. Bars **5-6** of the intro sequence the same pattern into the key of the modal dominant (Em), just as the melody at **A** will do. The difference here is that I only stay in Em for two measures instead of four. Bar **7** repeats bar **1** in Am.

Introducing the Breaks

Bars **4** and **8** are breaks. The first break is filled by the drums, and the second break (bar **8**) is silent. This sets up the form for letter **A**. Lots of things change between the intro and letter **A**, but the breaks, the bass melody, and the use of minor 2nds prepare us for what we are about to hear at **A**. We are surprised by the change of meter, the double time groove, and the horns taking over the orchestration. I was looking for surprise, but I also need some underlying continuity.

[Let's listen to the intro and letter **A**. You don't know it yet, but letter **B** will go back to the quarter-note groove (like the intro, except in 4/4). Shifting gears is a large part of the character of this piece.

When writing counterpoint, it is essential that we can hear each part clearly. Can you follow the clarinet part? The piccolo/piano part? The brass hits? The bass/bass clarinet part? The drums? There's a lot going on here. Clarity is of the utmost importance. We don't want to frustrate the listener.]

The *B* Theme

The purpose of a *B* theme is to contrast with the *A* theme. Opposites provide the starkest contrast. There also needs to be a subtle reference to the *A* section to provide continuity. Let's look at the contrasting elements.

- Rhythm: Rhumba vs. Arabic groove, relaxed quarter note pulse vs. agitated eighth note pulse, the melody moves in eighths and quarter notes while the backgrounds move more slowly using longer note values (predominantly half notes).
- Melody: New key (F vs. A), Mode (major vs. minor), scale-wise vs. grace notes and leaps, legato vs. articulated and jerky, romantic vs. impersonal.
- Harmony: Lush chords vs bare solos and unisons, chromatic jazz progressions and voicings vs. very basic tonic/dominant and modal progressions.
- Orchestration: Instrumentation (saxes vs. woodwind doubles, brass vs. no brass hits, Range (limited vs. expansive), Texture (melody/pad, thumb line).

As you can see, this *B* theme is about as different as I could make it. To reiterate: I didn't plan this or consciously devise the above points. I'm an intuitive arranger and composer. I just wrote what I heard in my head—what sounds good and is satisfying to me.

I started with the original melody for this section, imagined it being played romantically by the alto sax, subtly changed a rhythm or two to make it feel less predictable and then reharmonized it to enhance the romantic nature of the line. Once that was set, I proceeded to orchestrate the other horns, providing them with melodic parts that would enhance the mood of the melody, giving it more character.

I've been arranging for 60 years. In that time I've transcribed about 1000 charts to learn what other arrangers have done, and written well over 1000 of my own arrangements. When I started out, I learned all kinds of rules and tried to obey them but, little by little, I learned to trust my instincts more and more. When you do something often, after a while you stop thinking consciously about the details and focus more on big issues.

Transitions

Transitions are difficult to make sound convincing. We are moving from one idea to a contrasting idea. We need to make this sound inevitable. There are two basic approaches to transitions, smooth and abrupt. Either you want it to appear seamless, so the listener won't notice, or you want to surprise the listener. The transition in **A10** is a bit of both. Due to the drum break, it's mostly abrupt, but the three quarter note chords and the alto sax pickup prepare us for the new groove and key at **B**. Also, I added a bar to the form so that the drummer could play his break as before. I could have omitted the break and the extra measure, but that would feel *too* abrupt.

Adding and Subtracting Measures

Our experience playing music has beaten into us the importance of keeping the established form. This is essential for us to be in sync with the other performers. When we put on our arranger's hat, *we* determine the form. If we want to add or subtract measures, we simply tell the players in the written music. The key here is that the form should feel natural and not contrived.

Harmonizing Pickups

Very often pickups are not harmonized, leaving the harmony to start on the downbeat of the next section. This helps the listener to understand the form. Sometimes it's fun to cover up this seam with chromatic harmony, which is exactly what happens in the **bar before B** (see *Score* p. 4/p. 161).

The alto sax has two eighth-note pickups leading to a long note (half tied to an eighth), which take us from the faster eighth-note groove of letter **A** to the slower half-time rhumba groove of **B**. Just to complicate things, the other four horns play three quarter-note pickups to **B**, which make us feel a little like walking across a room on a ship while the waves beneath us are rolling at a different tempo—in other words, a bit unsettling.

Let's look at the harmony of these quarter-note pickups. We are approaching an Fmaj7 chord at **B**, so I'm going to work backwards using dominant approach—first C7, then its dominant (G7), and then A♭7 (the tritone sub of D7—the dominant of G7). Are you concerned about the relationship of A♭7 to the previous E7? I'm not. The A♭7 is a surprise. We have no idea what it means, until we follow the breadcrumbs for the next three chords.

Parallel Motion

Logically, I would think that the top line of these harmonies (the trumpet) should move in contrary motion to the alto pickup, thus creating an obvious set of opposites. Instead, I chose to give the trumpet an ascending line approaching the major 7th of the F chord at **B** (see *Score* p. 5/p. 162). This is really sneaky.

The trumpet ascends C, C#, D (half-steps). We expect the E to follow, but the trumpet drops out and the lower horns play the E down the octave—a downward leap of a minor 7th. Furthermore, the lower horns are now in unison rather than 4-part harmony. This change of texture further helps the listener understand the form.

Voicing from the Trumpet Down

Each of these three pickup voicings has the bari playing the roots on the bottom. On the A♭9 I've omitted the 5th, since it doesn't provide any color, and opted to use the 9th (Bb). The move to the G7-5 gives us contrary motion (two voices ascending vs. two descending—top up/bottom down).

Moving to the C7sus, we also have contrary motion (two ascending and two descending), but this time the first and third ascend, while the second and fourth descend. The use of the sus chord is to accommodate the F pickup in the alto. Dominant sus chords resolve smoothly to tonic major 7th chords (F on the C7 to E on the Fmaj7).

Stating the Melody of the B Theme

I'd like to keep the melody as simple and straightforward as possible. The original piece has the identical rhythm for each of the first three 2-bar phrases. That feels too predictable for my taste. How can I not disturb what's there and make it just a tad off-center? How about instead of using a pickup to each phrase, we begin the second and third phrase with the same pitches and rhythms but just displace it by a beat. That is; we'll start those phrases on the beat, rather than before the beat. It feels natural and adds a bit of charm.

Reharmonization

Rather than stick with the original *I vi ii V* chord progression, I'm going to dress it up just a bit. The E♭7 in **B2** is the tritone sub of A7 (the *V/vi*). This is especially nice since the alto melody for that bar is A (the ♭5 of E♭7).

I feel a need to add some harmonic interest to the three bars in the first ending (**B6-8**). What was originally C7 for three measures, I start with the C7 and end with it, but in between we take a little side trip.

Working backwards from the final C7-9 in **B8**, we have a Gm7-5, which sets up a *ii V* in F minor, thus creating a bit of melodrama, which gets relieved on the return of the Fmaj7 chord at **B**. The preceding Dm7 G7-9 is *ii V* into the C7 in **B8**. And finally, the A7 in **B6** is the dominant of the Dm7 in **B7**. I had the bassist walk down the F scale 5, 4, 3 to connect the C7 and A7 in **B6**.

Melody-bass Relationship

[This is all very smooth and supports the melody. Play just the alto sax melody and the bass part. Does it feel complete? Now we can add some inner parts that will add color to a solid structure.]

Alternating Thumb Lines with Harmonized Background Figures

Sometimes it's nice to accompany a melody with a thumb line. Sometimes it's nice to accompany a melody with harmonized pads or figures. Here is a passage that moves back and forth between the two.

Thumb Line Construction

Thumb lines avoid melody notes and bass notes to create a distinctive line and to combine with the melody and bass to convey the harmony. For chords of longer duration where the melody is not active, we often want to give some melodic motion to the thumb line. It is common to use 5, #5, 6, ♭7, major 7 and the root, either ascending or descending (chromatically or diatonically).

B1 goes from the major 7th to the 6th of the F major chord. The trumpet is tacet rather than have him double the line an octave higher, which might compete for attention with the alto sax melody.

B2 goes into harmony with the alto on the ♭5 and the lower horns on the 3rd, 7th, and root. This unstable chord (it contains two tritones—root/♭5 and 3rd/7th) provides a surprising contrast to the placid F major chord in **B1**.

B3-4 is an opportunity to move the thumb line. Starting on the 5th, it moves chromatically up to the 7th. The B♭ and B♮ have a lot of pull. They want to resolve. The upward direction of this chromatic line provides a satisfying opposite to the descending diatonic line in **B1**.

B5-6 combines the ascending 5, #5 of **B3** (transposed down a 5th to stay constant with the new chord change of Gm7) and the movement of thumb line to pad of **B1-2**.

We also are carrying on with the idea of switching back and forth from thumb line to pad. The alto and bari descend on the third beat of **B6**, while the tenor and bone hold their ♭9 and 7th. This happened because the alto moved down to the E (3rd of C7-9), and if I kept the bari on his E from the first two beats of the bar, they would be doubling each other at the octave. Moving the bari down to the root creates a more interesting relationship (minor 9th below the bone). The bassist plays a passing 7th (B♭) on beat 4 to make the move from C7 to Am7 smoother. Stepwise bass motion feels natural and logical.

In **B7**, pads continue but change chords at a faster pace (two beats each). Both the Am7 and A♭° half-note chords are voiced upwards root, 7th, 3rd. The alto moves in eighth notes stepwise alternating chord tones and tensions.

At **B8** it's back to unison for four eighth notes in an ascending Gm11-5 arpeggio (the B♭ in the alto is replaced by the C in the arpeggio to avoid agreement between foreground and background) and finally landing on a C7-9 pad.

The E in the tenor holds while the alto continues the upward line with his pickup into the repeat of **B**. If you are worried about the half-step between the tenor and the alto, just listen and see if it sounds okay. The reason we are not disturbed by this minor 2nd is that the trumpet note serves as the beginning of the alto pickup. Furthermore, the alto quickly resolves up a 2nd to the G, creating a very stable minor 3rd with the tenor.

Adding Dynamics

The crescendo into the *subito p* adds suspense to this semi-cadence. Dynamics add personality and expression to music. Don't overlook them. When I was young, all the older musicians played with a lot of expression—dynamics, accent, vibrato, etc. Working with them, I came to appreciate what they were doing and got in the habit of playing like that. These things pretty much went out of style with the advent of rock-and-roll-based pop music. Eliminating expression from music is self-defeating. I encourage these techniques, when appropriate.

The tradition in jazz has always been for players to add expression to their parts. Neither Duke Ellington nor Billy Strayhorn ever wrote any dynamics, vibrato, or accents in their music. They expected the players to interpret the parts and bring their own personalities to the music. With the advent of school bands and music published for amateur players, arrangers started writing dynamics, accents, slurs, vibrato, etc. This continues to this day. Most arrangers assume that whoever plays their music doesn't know jazz language enough to speak it authentically. I'm not big on enabling this level of ignorance. If players don't give you what you want, fix it at rehearsal. After a while, they will get the hang of it, and make your music theirs.

In general, my parts give the players the information that they don't know or wouldn't know. I'd like to encourage their participation as much as possible. Not all arrangers agree with my approach. Many put a dynamic, accent, and slur on every single note. I've noticed that the more you write on the parts, the less the players pay attention to what you've written. If you put accents on every note or every other note, which is pretty much how we play, players won't play with *any* accent. If you write only the accents the players wouldn't necessarily know about, they are more likely to give you what you want.

Repetition and Surprise

B1-5 is interesting enough to bear repetition. This helps the listener and players alike. When we get to the sixth bar of the phrase, I feel that we need a surprise—any more repetition will seem dull to the listener. We need to keep everyone on their toes. They need to know that at any moment something new and exciting might happen.

Red Herrings

The Em7-5/A, which is essentially an A7sus4-9, makes us think that we are going to Dm, but instead I slid down another half-step to D♭9 (♭VI9 in F). This is a traditional spot for a shoulder chord—setting up a cadence. Rather than going to a second-inversion tonic and then the dominant, I simplified and went directly to the dominant (C7-9).

Romance

All these -9 and m7-5 chords add an element of romance that contrasts starkly with the Arabic vibe of the intro and letter **A**.

More Suspense

The C7-9 is held for an extra measure rather than resolving to the tonic. We finally get the tonic at the beginning of the new section at **C**. While we hold out this dominant, the Harmon-muted trumpet soloist enters early. The dovetailing of phrases covers up seams in the music and adds continuity.

Choreography

Notice that the trumpet has all of letter **B** to add the mute. It's always important to choreograph mute and instrument changes. Duke Ellington said that he liked to give his soloists eight bars before and after a solo to give the players time to walk to and from the solo microphone. This is a good idea, since most players will omit their written parts just before and after a solo anyway.

Shifting Gears in the Rhythm Section

The rhythm section is given the responsibility to set up the swing groove that is coming up at **C**. I know what I want the bassist to play. I'd rather leave it up to the pianist and drummer to improvise their own solutions. The more I can get the rhythm section to function as they do in a trio, the better. Sometimes I need to assign them specific notes to support what is going on in the horns and/or to avoid chaos, but mostly I like to encourage their creativity.

[Let's examine what's going on in letter **B** (see *Score* p. 5/p. 162). First, go to the piano and play each individual part along with the bass part. Did everyone get a satisfying line to play? Billy Strayhorn would always ask the players if they liked their part.

Now, listen to letter **B**. Is it convincing as a romantic passage? Can you picture the table for two with the linen tablecloth and two lit candles?

Next, listen from the top of the chart up to **C**. Is there enough contrast between sections? Does it hold together as a piece? Are the transitions convincing, or do they feel contrived? And, finally, are we dying to hear where this story is going?]

Solos

Choosing What Material to Develop

Following the intro, *A* theme, and *B* theme, I feel it's time to develop the previous material. The question is: Which material? I could go back to the Arabic groove or do something else with the A minor form, or I could use the F major progression to develop, saving the A minor Arabic groove for the recapitulation.

A minor offers a more modal approach, which puts demands on the soloists to create harmonic interest since the rhythm section is so reserved. The F major option offers a more diatonic/chromatic progression that provides the soloists with a lot of low-hanging fruit. I didn't feel like I'd had enough of the F major material in the exposition, so I chose to develop that.

Avoiding Repeats Within Repeats

Letters **C** through **D** (see *Score* pp. 6-7/pp. 161-162) are open for solos. It's a 16-bar chorus based on the form of letter **B**. I was able to use a repeat in **B**, but since this section is going to repeat for trumpet, tenor, and then piano, and each player will play one or more choruses, it would be too confusing to write 8 bars with a first and second ending and then have a repeat within a repeat. Definitely not kosher.

Start with the Chord Progression

I wrote the changes from **B** for the piano and bass and 4/4 swing in the drums. I don't need to tell the pianist and bassist what to comp for the soloists or what to

CJCA III: WRITING FOR SMALL GROUPS

Example 10-1 In A Persian Market octet score, page 1

IN A PERSIAN MARKET – OCTET ARRANGEMENT

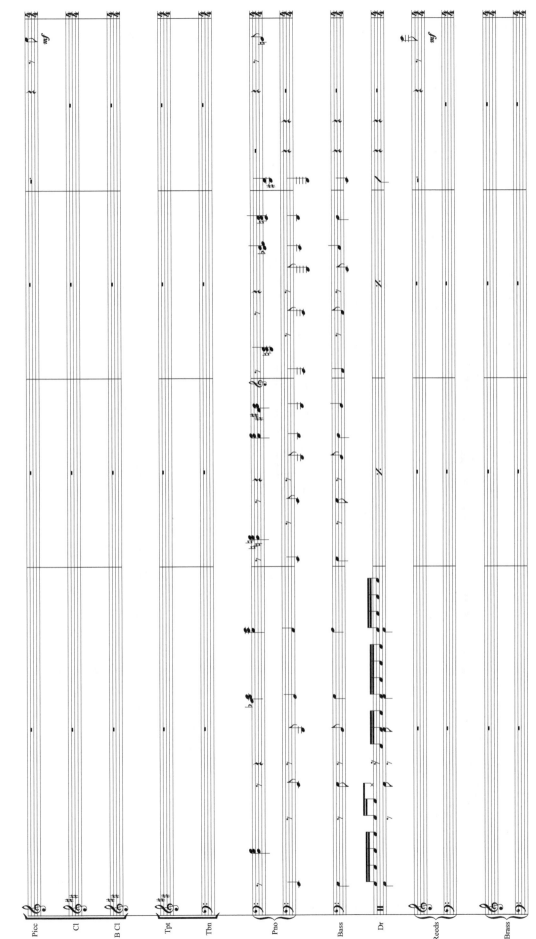

Example 10-1 In A Persian Market octet score, page 2

CJCA III: WRITING FOR SMALL GROUPS

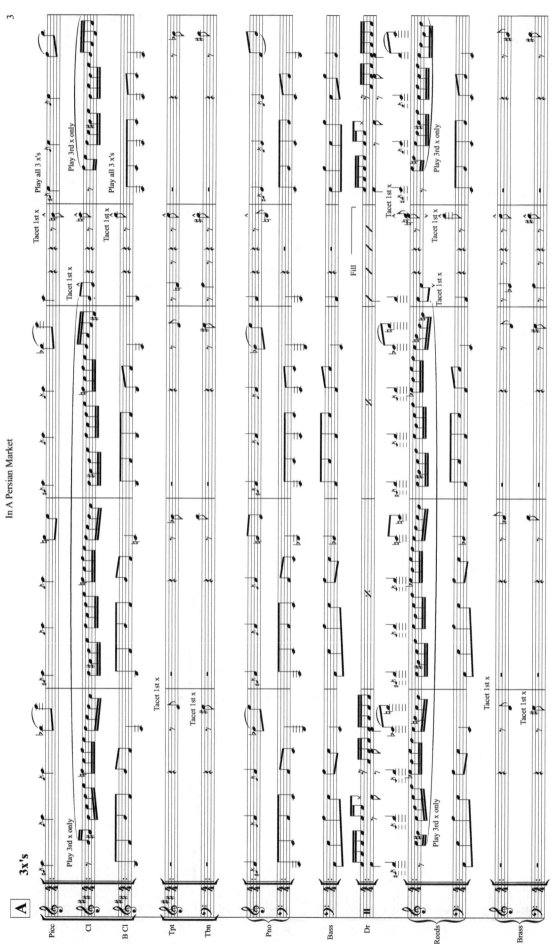

Example 10-1 In A Persian Market octet score, page 3

IN A PERSIAN MARKET – OCTET ARRANGEMENT

Example 10-1 In A Persian Market octet score, page 4

CJCA III: WRITING FOR SMALL GROUPS

Example 10-1 In A Persian Market octet score, page 5

IN A PERSIAN MARKET – OCTET ARRANGEMENT

Example 10-1 *In A Persian Market* octet score, page 6

CJCA III: WRITING FOR SMALL GROUPS

Example 10-1 In A Persian Market octet score, page 7

IN A PERSIAN MARKET – OCTET ARRANGEMENT

Example 10-1 In A Persian Market octet score, page 8

CJCA III: WRITING FOR SMALL GROUPS

Example 10-1 In A Persian Market octet score, page 9

Example 10-1 In A Persian Market octet score, page 10

CJCA III: WRITING FOR SMALL GROUPS

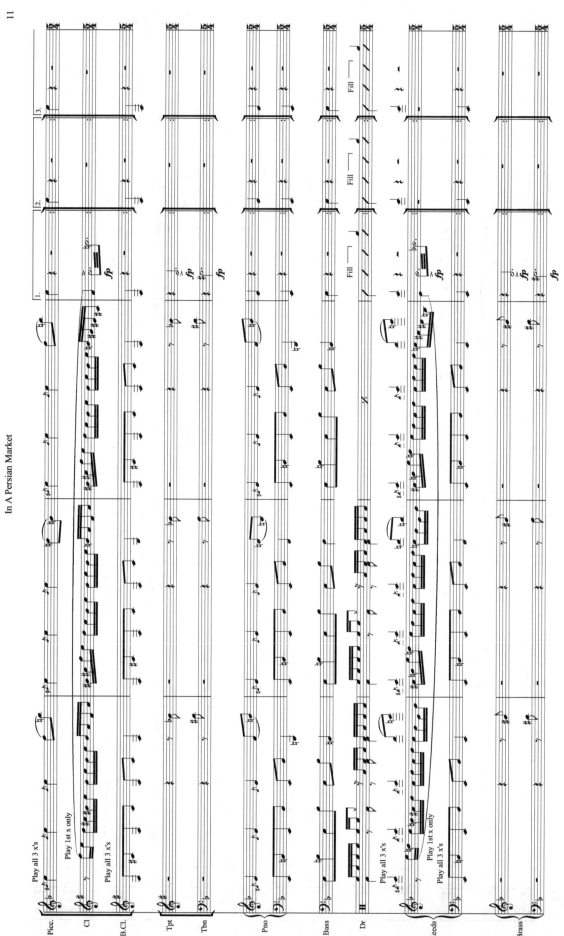

Example 10-1 *In A Persian Market* octet score, page 11

IN A PERSIAN MARKET – OCTET ARRANGEMENT

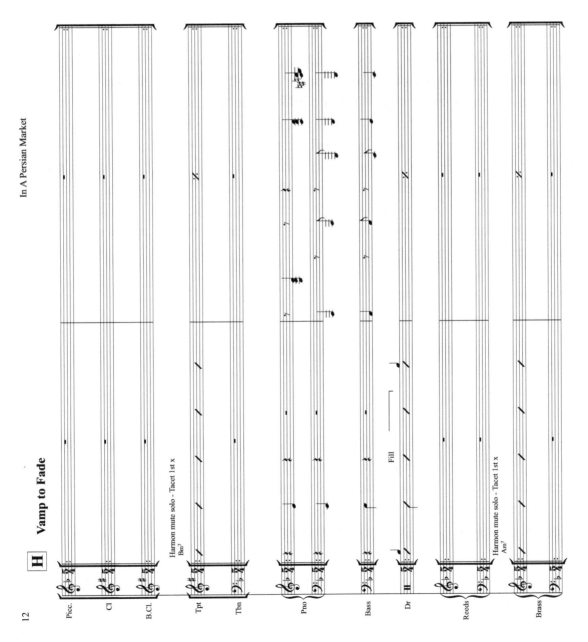

Example 10-1 *In A Persian Market* octet score, page 12

play on their solos. I want improvised interaction between the soloists and the rhythm section.

Creating Backgrounds for Soloists

The two basic purposes of backgrounds for solos are:

- To make the soloist sound good.
- To keep the soloist (and everyone else) in the game (furthering the development of the motifs).

I'm careful not to let the backgrounds be too busy; that would crowd the soloist. In a call-and-response situation, I can get fancier, but otherwise, my approach is to write the types of things I would play if I were comping on piano. The difference is that if I were comping, I would be following the soloist's lead. When you write a background, it is played the same way each time, and the soloist must respond to it.

When to Add the Background

In this solo section, I wrote a background for the remaining four horns to be played under the trumpet solo. I'm leaving it up to the performers to decide which trumpet chorus gets the background. It could be the first, second, third, etc. It depends on how many choruses he'll play, and when it will feel most satisfying to add this element. Do we want to start off with this rich texture and then be more spare (just rhythm section), do we want to start spare, add the richness, and then go back to the sparseness of the rhythm section, or should we leave the background for the final trumpet chorus—building to a climax and following it with a new soloist (the tenor)? I'm going to leave this decision for when we rehearse, or even when we perform. It could be different every time.

Possible Background Textures

The four textures commonly used for backgrounds are:

- Rhythmic figures
- Pads
- Thumb lines
- Riffs.

For this chorus I will be using the first three textures. **C1-4** is a rhythmic figure, **C5-6** is a pad, **C7-9** is a thumb line. Similarly, **D1-4** is the same rhythmic figure (cut and paste), **D5-7** is a pad, and **D8** is a thumb line. Changing textures gives me variety to make up for the rhythmic simplicity. I also used rich harmonies to keep the listener interested and to goose the soloist just a bit.

Don't forget the use of rests. They can be surprising, and at the very least, they give us time to digest the written material. If it is complex, we will need this time to understand and appreciate what we are hearing.

Everyone plays a melody.

Even though the focal point in this section is the soloist, I want each player to have an interesting and rewarding part to play. It's like when we watch a football game. One rainy day when I was in junior high, our gym coach played us a film of a college football game. He stopped the camera and asked us what we saw. We told him that the quarterback handed the ball off to the fullback, who then ran it for a touchdown. He then told us to watch the play again. It was at that moment that we realized that the fullback in the film was our very own coach, playing seven or eight years earlier.

Now we were really focused on the fullback carrying the ball! Coach Maushart then pointed to two defensive linemen. He instructed us to watch them. He explained that they created the hole through which he could run with the ball. That was what made the play work, and enabled the touchdown. As sports fans and jazz fans, we often are distracted by the foreground and miss the important catalysts in the background.

That said, everyone involved in creating the background should have a fun part to play. It needs to be functional in supporting the soloist (and not distracting us), but it should also contain such good elements of rhythm, melody, harmony and orchestration that it could stand on its own and hold our interest.

Creating Lead Lines

At this point, I was mostly focused on creating a good melody for the alto sax, since that's who would be playing the top part in the background. I've already got the harmonies in place, so the alto will conform to those chords while developing melodic (and possibly rhythmic) material from letter **B**.

To be honest, I wasn't thinking about developing anything for the alto. I just wrote him a part that seemed interesting while being supportive. My subconscious did the rest of the work. Until this very moment of writing, I haven't given any thought to how the alto melody relates to letter **B**. Let's see how I did.

Analyzing the Melody at Letter B

Here are the basic pitches:

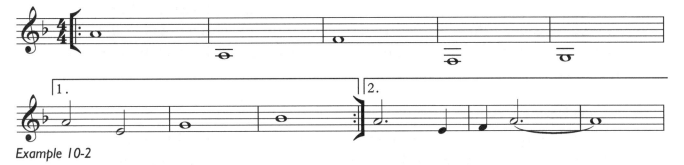

Example 10-2

I've eliminated all the auxiliary pitches, so that we can more readily see the shape of the line. Pretty attractive, right? The auxiliary pitches are comprised of 2nds, with the exception of the downward perfect 5th (E to A) and back up a perfect 4th (A to D) from **B1-3**, the Dm downward arpeggio **B3-4**, upward perfect 5th and downward perfect 4th, the upward leap of a 4th (D to A) from **B5-6**, and then the perfect 4th drop (A to E) in **B6** and **B9**, the minor 6th leap (D to B) from **B7-8**, and the perfect 4th drop in **B8**. All these wide intervals give the melody character. Notice that they are almost exclusively perfect 4ths and 5ths.

Creating a Strong Background Melody

Let's go back to letter **C** and examine the alto line. The first two notes (E jumping down to A in **C1**) form a downward leap of a perfect 5th. **C3** is a downward leap of a perfect 4th. We've established the characteristic intervals. Incidentally, perfect 4ths are the inversions of perfect 5ths.

Hidden and Exposed Ascending Lines

Let's do a little Schenker-inspired analysis of the alto line in **C** and **D**.

Example 10-3

What we are looking at is an ascending line that goes through the changes. All these notes appear in the alto part, except for the Db and D♮ in measures **6** and **14**, where the line is handed off temporarily to the trombone (second voice).

Natural Resolutions of 3rds and 7ths

In jazz, many, if not most, harmonies are made up of dominant 7th chords resolving around the circle of 5ths or down a half-step, or *ii V* progressions. Mostly, the tendency is for downward resolutions of the 3rds and 7ths of these chords. It feels satisfying to counter these downward resolutions with upward chromatic and diatonic lines, hence the line in **C** and **D**. It feels like it is defying gravity, which in a way, it is.

Creating Harmony Parts

I'm not going to worry about the other three horns yet. Basically, I'll fill out the harmonies creating voicings that sound good to me vertically while making pleasing melodies for each instrument. I wrote all of these harmony parts intuitively; whatever sounded good to my ear is what went on the page. I keep in mind the mood and aesthetic of letter **B**. I want to continue that but now in a swing context.

4-Part Harmony

One of the nice things about having five horns in an ensemble is that if one horn is soloing, the others can create 4-part harmony. These rich voicings can be written in close harmony, open harmony or semi-close harmony (Drop 2 or Drop 3). The entire passage can be homogeneous, or we can move from one to another. Let's see what happened:

C1: close to open		**D1**: close to open
C2: rest		**D2**: rest
C3: close		**D3**: close
C4: rest		**D4**: rest
C5: open		**D5**: open
C6: Drop 2		**D6**: Drop 2
C7: open		**D7**: close to open
C8: unison thumb line		**D8**: unison thumb line

Creating Inner Voices

Once my lead line (alto) is in place over the chord changes, I'm just going to let my intuition guide me to what sounds good in the voicings. The above graph of textures was unknown to my conscious mind during the writing process. It's just what felt right to me. The same goes for the alterations in the chords and the individual lines that the other three horns play (as usual, I suggest playing each line in conjunction with the roots in the bass).

I was merely trying to capture the essence of the song without specifically stating the melody. This structure evolved out of many years of listening to, playing, and studying great music. I didn't set out to copy anyone or anything—it was just me having a conversation with an imaginary soloist. Of course, it doesn't hurt to analyze our work after the fact. The more you understand, the more sinks into your subconscious mind for future use.

[Let's listen to this solo section (**C** and **D**). Does it make you want to improvise a line over it? I hope so. After all, the main purpose is to inspire the soloist. Now let's listen to the chart from the top up to letter **E**. At the end of the solo section, are you feeling a desire to hear everyone play together and complete the development of the material? If so, then we will be ready to move on.]

The Shout Chorus

I hesitate to call this ensemble chorus a "shout chorus" because it doesn't shout. The term "shout chorus" comes from swing charts of the 1930s, where the entire big band shouts swinging rhythms. The entire band playing f or $f\!f$

feels exhilarating to both dancers and listeners alike. It's the culmination of the development of the motif(s) of the piece.

Since this is neither a big band (small groups have adopted this term) nor a swing chart (letters **E** and **F** switch back to the rhumba of letter **B**), "shout" seems inappropriate, since the mood is more mellow and introspective than shouting. Shout choruses are sometimes called "sock choruses," but that too doesn't seem to help. What we have here is a sophisticated concerted/contrapuntal statement of the melody that uses an instrumentation similar to the Arabic theme of letter **A** to unify the disparate elements of **A** and **B**.

With a Nod to Quincy Jones and Gil Evans

In the 1950s and '60s, Quincy Jones and Gil Evans pioneered the integration of flutes and other woodwind doubles into the mainstream of jazz. To create this cool, yet complex vibe, I had the flute play the melody with the clarinet, Harmon-muted trumpet and cup-muted trombone in concerted 4-part harmony below. In opposition, the unison bass clarinet, piano and string bass play a counter-line, which is, in essence, a dressed-up bass line including lots of chord roots. We will get back to the bass part in a little while. As for the drums, all I need from him is a basic rhumba pattern that won't interfere with the complex counterpoint between the harmonized melody and bass clarinet, piano, and string bass.

Orchestrating for Flute

Although the flute has a 3-octave range (middle C to C above high C), the extreme registers aren't applicable for this passage. The bottom octave and a 4th will not project enough to be heard above the other horns. Conversely, the top eight notes would be too shrill for the mellow blend I'm after in this section. The clarinet is able to blend easily with the flute and to avoid overpowering it.

What to Do with the Brass

Both the trumpet and trombone are louder instruments which, in the hands of seasoned, sensitive professionals, can blend with the flute. An easier blend is to put the brass in mutes, which brings their volume into balance with the flute, thus enabling me to use the octave in the staff going down to F. Mutes also change the color of the brass instruments greatly, making them closer in tone to the flute.

Harmonizing Pickups

As I said before, it's common to not harmonize pickups. They can be played solo, in unison, or in octaves, saving the harmony to begin on the next downbeat. This helps to define the form.

Another approach is to harmonize pickups; creating tension and release (at the tonic chord on the downbeat. In this case, the usual procedure is to harmonize the pickup with the dominant 7th chord of the key. Often pickups outline the tonic chord, making a dominant harmonization a bit tricky. The tonic note would be the sus4 of the *V7*. I've seen and heard these types of pickups harmonized with tonic chords. This may not work all the time because the tonic pickup can give away the punchline before the downbeat of the form.

Embracing the Dark Side

The bar before **E** (see *Score* p. 7/p. 164) as the flute melody 5, 1, 2 in the key of F. My initial thought was to harmonize all three notes with C7sus4 chords, however this harmony sounded bland and lacked sufficient darkness. This not-really-a-shout chorus needs to fully develop the ideas and aesthetic of the entire piece. I'm choosing to use the melodic, harmonic, and rhythmic framework of the *A* (Arabic minor key) theme.

My orchestration (use of flute, clarinet, bass clarinet, and muted brass) reminds us of the *A* theme, but that's not enough. I feel a need to address the darkness of that minor strain and contrast it with the F major key, overall chord progression and diatonic melody, so that dark and light will coexist as they do in real life.

The target chord is the Fmaj7 on the downbeat of letter **E** (see *Score* p. 8/p. 165). With the 3rd in the melody, this will undoubtedly be the brightest voicing. C7sus4 doesn't give me an opposite (dark) pickup, which I crave to make the Fmaj7 feel satisfying. Possible dominant substitutes are:

♭*II*	G♭7	Tritone sub
ivm	B♭m	The chord of despair
♭*VII7*	E♭7	
VII7	E7	Leading tone dominant
IV7	B♭7	plagal cadence

Opting for the Churchy Plagal Cadence

The tritone sub doesn't work because of the conflict of the melody notes F and G, but all the other possible chords could work. E7 is a bit dicey, but possible. I actually thought of B♭7 first, and just stayed with that. The A9+5 passing chord on beat 4 is a leading tone dominant to the B♭13 on the *and*-of-4 used to avoid repeated notes in the lower parts and create stronger voice leading (inner melodies).

Creating Consistency in a Complex Whirlwind of Changing Harmonies

To offset the surprising harmonies in the shout chorus, I needed a few elements to ground it. First is the basic repetitive rhumba drum pattern coupled with the same orchestration throughout this section—woodwind/muted brass 4-part harmony opposed by bass clarinet/piano/string bass unison counterpoint—basic harmonic progression from letter **B**. The use of the **B** melody is certainly comforting and unifying, but I needed one more subtle element. To keep the sound consistent, I voiced nearly every chord in Drop 2.

The Usual Disclaimer

I reiterate, none of the information in this section was known to me on a conscious level while creating the music. I only realized it while analyzing years later in the writing of this book. This sort of stuff is intuitive for most composers and arrangers. I've noticed it in other arrangers' work, but each piece has different needs, so there is no one formula that fits all. I believe it's best to follow one's instincts. Of course, if those instincts are preceded by years of listening, playing, and studying, more and better options can come to mind.

Parallel vs. Contrary Motion

Oh yes, there is one more constant element—parallel motion. The diatonic 2nds of the melody most naturally suggested diatonic planing (diatonic approach) for the harmonies. I pitted that against the bass part, which opposes the melody both rhythmically and in direction, as much as possible. The more different the shapes of these two disparate elements, the more clearly they will be defined as opposites. They need to be at war with each other so that the ultimate truce will feel sweet.

Hold Onto Your Hats

I should warn you; we are about to dissect some complicated harmonies. Although I'm generally linked with Duke Ellington's music, one of my other big influences has been Gil Evans. I actually worked as Gil's copyist for a few months when I was young. One day I asked Gil about his aesthetic. He surprised me by saying that he just wanted his music to sound like Billy Strayhorn's.

It took me a minute to wrap my brain around that, but after a while, it started to make sense. Keeping in mind the deep relationship between Strayhorn and Ellington, it's not that farfetched that I would be attracted to Gil's music, although I see them as the two sides of my brain—both beautiful, but aesthetically opposite.

Duke is sensual and earthy; Gil is more remote, less emotional and very sophisticated and intellectual. Duke described himself as primitive. Strays and Gil were sophisticates. Each strove to incorporate their opposites. For my money, Duke was the most successful at integrating both, but it's a close call. For me, this is as good as jazz composition gets.

Contrary Motion

Contrary motion only occurs in the inner parts on the first pickup (to create a nice melody in the bottom part and a minor 2nd with the part above it), in **E7** on the *and*-of-3 (to create a minor 2nd between the second and third part), and in **F5** (on the *and*-of-3 to create a minor 2nd between the second and third part, and on the following note to create a major 7th between the first and third parts, and moving to the last note of the bar to get us back to the m9/maj7 voicings that are so prevalent and create so much character). Minor 2nd and major 7th intervals generate tension. They add spice. Many of the voicings in this section contain these intervals. They offset all the relatively bland m7 chords. This dichotomy of dissonance gives us the tension and release so essential to drama.

Laying the Groundwork

The first thing I wrote at letter **E** is the melody in the flute. I never wrote the basic changes (from letter **B**), but I knew what they were. When harmonizing the flute melody, I kept in mind the roots of those basic chords, even though I didn't write them out. I knew the bass part would be more active melodically. Before I added the bass part, I went on to write the flute part for letter **F** (see *Score* p. 9/p. 166).

Taking it further out, but keeping us grounded

I haven't done this often, but it's a great concept that I've heard Strayhorn and Ellington do—when restating a melody, keep the shape of the melody and the basic chord structure, but use different melody notes. The flute part at **F** has the same shape as **E** but is a 5th higher; it's in the key of C, but everyone else remains in the key of F. This bitonality will add a serious amount of interest and tension. Because the keys of F and C are very closely related, the amount of dissonance is only slightly more than the previous eight bars; just enough to sound interesting without being shocking. It's a bit like modulating, but it doesn't affect the structure of the chart like a key change would.

Now it's time to write the Bass Counterpoint

My parameters are:
- Use roots and fifths.
- Stay away from the flute notes.
- Make the rhythms as different from the horns as possible.
- Move at a different pace when possible.
- Make the shapes of the lines as different as possible. Employ contrary motion.

Good counterpoint means creating two or more interdependent melodies.
Each must be able to stand on its own and yet complement the other. In free counterpoint (not imitative), I try to give each line a different character. The main thing we are striving for is forward motion through teamwork. While adhering to all these imperatives, do not lose track of the motif(s). Keep developing them. Use prior material. My favorite spot in the bass part is the 16th notes in **E4**. There are a few other 16ths in the line, but this is the only time the figure in **B10** comes back.

Transitioning Back to A Minor

The jazz waltz at **F7-10** provides a transition back to the A minor Arabic groove of letter **A**. Although the chord progression is essentially a series of chromatically descending dominant 7ths, both the top piano notes and the bass notes are rife with perfect 4ths—one last shot at the 5th/4th characteristic interval of the *B* theme. The piano left hand consists of descending tritones (the 3rds and 7ths of each chord);

leaving the roots for the bassist and the tensions (13, b5, b5, 9) to the right hand. The final Bb13 resolves smoothly down a half-step to Am.

But why the waltz?

Maybe that's a reference to the 5/4 intro. 5/4 is a waltz plus half a 4/4 bar. It always sounds like a three-legged waltz to me. In any event, this 4-bar transition sets up the following Arabic groove as well as foreshadowing the return of the 5/4 groove.

[Let's look at this shout chorus as a whole. I suggest you go to the piano and play each horn part in conjunction with the root of the basic chord progression (written above the bottom stave of the reduction). Does each line make a good melody? I recommend that you always put the inside melodies in your charts to this test. If there are melodic issues, make adjustments. That's what erasers were made for.

Now, listen to letters **E** and **F** including the pickup to **E**. Granted, this is complex, but it shouldn't sound weird. When we get to the bitonality at **F**, it should feel like we kicked into a higher gear.

Just to be clear, shout choruses almost never repeat the melody verbatim. This is a rare instance where it worked. Perhaps the reason is the *ABA* multi-themed structure. The best thing is that it saved me from having to create new material. The piece is more concise and understandable because this melody came back. It's sort of a combination shout and recapitulation of the *B* theme.

Let's go back and listen to the entire chart from the beginning up to letter **G**. Does this multi-strain piece hang together? Does is develop enough to feel satisfying? Are we ready to go home (recapitulation)?]

Recapitulation and Coda

At this point, I'm done writing. It's all copy and paste from here. Letter **G** is the same as **A**, except that the repeats are played in the opposite order, so that instead of adding instruments for each repetition, instruments are subtracted. (see *Score* p. 10/p. 167). It ends with a drum fill that transitions to **H**, the 2-bar vamp coda (the first two bars of the intro). The trumpet gets two bars rest and time to put in his Harmon, and move closer to the mic for his solo over the vamp. Trumpet was an easy choice for soloist, since he soloed earlier in the chart.

In recording, we used a board fade. For live performance we would add an extra A quarter-note downbeat to give a feeling of finality.

[Let's listen to the chart in its entirety. How do you feel about the arc of the piece? It's a musical palindrome—intro, *A*, *B*, solos, *B*, *A*, intro. Neat and tidy. I've tried in subtle ways to make it unpredictable. Now that you've looked at it under a microscope, does it hold interest for you, or do you need more surprises? Every piece of music is a balancing act.]

11. Careless Love
Octet Arrangement

Finally, here's a sweet little dessert in the tradition the wonderful 4-horn charts that Ray Charles recorded for Atlantic in the 1950s. I've also incorporated some New Orleans groove and Ellington pep section (I'll explain soon) plunger work—all in the service of creating a setting for a fun vocal. In the tradition of the blues (this is not a 12-bar blues, but it utilizes blues melodies, rhythms, harmonies, and orchestration), **Careless Love** is a sad story told in a joyful, life-affirming manner. Life is hard and often cruel, but the sun will shine on my backdoor someday.

Eyes on the Prize

The focus of every vocal chart is telling the story. All the music is in service to the words and the singer's performance of those words. It's of utmost importance that every word of the lyric be heard and understood. Our instrumental accompaniment should be interesting, but never upstage the vocal. Our job as arrangers is to make the singer sound good and help him/her tell the story.

Jazz is a Conversation

Although there are basic pitches and rhythms notated for the vocal, I fully expect (and want) the vocalist not to be literal. In the tradition of the blues, the melody should be sung in a conversational manner. This can be done in many ways, as demonstrated in recordings of this song by Bessie Smith, Billie Holiday, Jimmy Rushing, Dinah Washington, Ray Charles, and Nat Cole, and many others.

Constants and Variables

My point of view is that the words are sacred. I go back as far as I can to find the original words and don't mess with them. They are timeless poetry. Even when they use bad grammar or refer to things and places that no longer exist, I want to conjure up that world. This is part of their charm. Before I write one note, I go back to the source to learn the original words, melody, and chord progression. I'll take some liberties with the melody and even more with the harmony, but the words are sacred to me.

Trusting My Judgment

Even if some of the aforementioned singers changed some of the words, I'm going with the lyric I know is original. If I do make any changes (I didn't with this song), it is in the spirit of capturing the original flavor of the story. On the other hand, I feel that it is incumbent on the arranger to create a unique instrumental setting for the story that honors its roots but is relevant today. I don't want my music to sound dated, either now or in the future. Unlike pop art, which is stuck in the era of its creation (mid- to late-1950s), great art is timeless and transcends its moment of creation.

Form and Authorship

Careless Love has a 16-bar *aaba* form. Although W.C. Handy is credited as the composer, he often wrote down and codified the songs he heard others singing.

Careless Love probably originated as an 18th-century English ballad, brought to our shores by English or Scotch-Irish settlers. In the folk version, the girl's pregnancy (the result of careless love!) causes her lover to abandon her. Folklorist Alan Lomax wrote, "In my opinion mountain songs like *Careless Love* provided the mould into which (Mississippi) Delta singers poured their free, bluesy hollers."

W.C. Handy, who said he heard a variation of the song in Bessemer, Alabama around 1892, actually published it as *two* blues songs with different lyrics, *Loveless Love* and *Careless Love*. After publication, we have recordings that show how these songs were performed over a period of more than a century.

The *a* section (**A1-4**, **A5-8**, **B5-8**) is all tonic and dominant:

$\| I | V | I | I | I | V | V | V \|$, and $\| I | V | I | I \|$

The *b* section (**B1-4**) is more like the blues (an abbreviated form of bars 3-6 of the blues, to be precise):

$| I | V/IV | IV | \#ivo |$

As in the blues, the *#ivo* could also be a *ivm*. Both accommodate this melody equally well and are fun to blow on. I pretty much went with the diminished chord in this chart, except at **J4**, where I used an A♭7 (♭*VII7* sub for the *ivm*).

Choosing a Key

Since the vocalist is the primary focus of this chart, I asked our singer if she knew the song; and if so, what key she wanted to sing it in. Every singer has a unique instrument. They will choose keys to accommodate their range and to place certain syllables and words in their voice to get a special sound or effect. Often, they can sing a song in several keys, but one key is usually the best for them. Singers who also play the piano will find their keys. Those who don't play instruments usually work with an accompanist to find the right key.

I've been lucky to work with many top singers over the past 50 years. Since I was in high school, I haven't had to help anyone find their key. When writing an arrangement of *I'm Beginning To See The Light* for Natalie Cole for the Grammys, I spoke with her on the phone and asked what key she would like. To my surprise,

s009
she said she didn't know! (Maybe she was too busy to look it up?) She asked me to just use the key from her prior recording of it. I guess she had a musical director who took care of those things for her, and she trusted that I would likewise know what to do.

Getting Started

I printed out my score paper with my octet template (see my book ***Streamlined Sibelius**®*), adding an extra stave for the vocal. Vocals are traditionally written either at the top of the score page or just above the rhythm section; I prefer the latter. Then, I inserted the meter and key signatures, and put in the title, and copyright information. I left a free page for the intro, since that would probably come later, once the chart revealed its intro to me. Then I wrote out the vocal part twice. There are three sets of lyrics for this song. I figured I'd use the first two at the top of the chart, and save the third for the out head.

Devising the Drum Part and Bass Line

My overarching idea for this chart was to put an interesting groove on the first chorus, and then go into 4/4 swing. I had the drums play eighth notes with sticks on the rims, while playing a heartbeat on the bass drums. He can repeat this infectious beat for the entire chorus. At the same time, I'd like the bass (doubled in the piano left hand) to play a syncopated line that makes good counterpoint with the vocal. The piano and bass should feel complete with just those two elements—the drums and horns are the gravy for this dish.

The Blues

I took the liberty of using the ♭7 on the tonic (we often do this when we play the blues) right away in **A1**, rather than waiting to introduce it in **B2**, where it normally appears in this song.

Rhythmic Displacement

I wanted the bass line to be repetitive, but at the same time, surprising. I accomplished this by displacing the entrances of the bass motif (the first five notes in **A1**; see *Score* p. 2,/p. 189). The first repeat of the motif starts on the *and*-of-4 of that measure. It's based on the *V* chord (F7) rather than on the tonic (B♭7) and adds an extra syncopation at the end as a kind of exclamation point.

A3 repeats the 5-note motif of **A1**, but instead of moving on to the dominant, it repeats on the tonic with the same displacement. In **A4** the exclamation point elides with the start of a new iteration of **A1**, this time displaced, so that it starts on the *and*-of-3 and ends with two extra dominant (F) exclamation points on the beat.

A6 has two beats of B♭ (no 7th) and two of B°, which leads into F7. If you are worried about the upward chromatic bass line (B♭ B°) not resolving up to C (either a Cm7 or a second inversion F7, the C occurs in the bass on beat 2 of **A7** and, even better, a beat earlier in the vocal. The roots and 5ths in **A5-6** are fragments of the **A1** motif. **A7-8** is the **A1-2** motif but all on F7 instead of B♭7 to F7.

B1-2 (see *Score* p. 3/p. 190) is more fragments of **A1**; **B3** is the motif transposed to E♭7, and **B4** comes to rest on E (the root of E°). **B5-6** is a cut and paste of **A1-2**. **B7-8** is the motif with the displaced repetition remaining on B♭7.

Describing this is actually much more complicated that the music sounds. That's the point—it feels natural.

The Pep Section

Duke Ellington's late 1920s band had three brass: two trumpets and a trombone. One of the trumpet players (Bubber Miley) introduced Duke to the plunger mute. Bubber heard King Oliver use it, and quickly became a master. Trombonist "Tricky" Sam Nanton learned plunger technique from Miley. Often, they would play in 3rds or 6ths, using inflections to emulate the human voice.

After a while the other trumpet player (Arthur Whetsol) was pressed into service to form triadic harmony. This trio remained an Ellington orchestrational staple long after Miley's and Nanton's early demises.

Duke's name for the trio of plunger-muted brass was the "pep section." The term has stuck and can be expanded to include the duo of trumpet and trombone in plungers. To be authentic, you want to use a plug inside the bells, producing a pinched sound in addition to making the pitch more controllable and diminishing the volume (thereby requiring the players to play with more force, resulting in greater intensity).

Call-and-Response

The scheme for **A** is for the brass to be in call-and-response with the saxes (two bars apiece). They should be as opposite as possible. The brass needs to travel at a different pace from the vocal. Since the vocal is mostly quarter notes, the brass is in half notes. Also, to keep the brass and vocal independent from each other, it's a good idea to give them different pitches and different shapes to their lines.

Everyone Wants to Play a Strong Melody

Within those parameters, my first concern is creating an effective melodic line for the trumpet, since he has the top voice and therefore will be more noticeable than the trombone. If I remember correctly, I wrote the brass notes simultaneously, making sure each instrument got a strong melody that defined the chord progression without doubling any of the vocal pitches.

CARELESS LOVE – OCTET ARRANGEMENT

Variation and Prioritizing

This worked out well for **A1-4**, but on the next four bars, I needed to vary the brass parts for the sake of interest. The F in the trumpet necessitated me writing a D for the trombone, which doubles the vocal. A lower pitch for the trombone would yield a less attractive line for him. *When it comes to musical priorities, melody trumps harmony.*

Remember the four elements of music?

Rhythm, Melody, Harmony, Orchestration—in that order.

Sax Answers

Now let's look at the sax responses at **A**. As opposed to the on-the-beat long notes in the brass, the saxes play in groups of two notes: a legato pickup to a short downbeat in sync with the bass drum. Each downbeat is voiced root, 3rd, 7th for the B♭7s, and root 7th, 3rd for the F7s, thus only moving the top two voices up a half-step. The pickups are all chromatic lower neighbors and are voiced parallel. In addition to answering the brass, the saxes also answer the vocal. This happens twice. The third time, the 2-note pattern is played quickly in succession removing the previous rest.

The Intro

As soon as I wrote the sax lick in **A3-4**, I recognized the potential it had as an introduction. I didn't want to tell too much of the story, so for the intro, I gave the sax parts to the piano with answers from the drums (see *Score* p. 1/p. 188). The 2-bar figure then repeats. This sets up letter **A** without giving away the melody, the groove, the brass, or the words. Although the sax figure is attractive, it doesn't spoil any of the surprise when we hear the melody. In fact, we congratulate ourselves for understanding its familiarity when it does return in the saxes at **A3**.

The Bridge

I need to change the structure at letter **B** (see *Score* p. 3/p. 190). This is the 4-bar bridge of the song. The bridge of any song needs to contrast with the *a* section. The bass line at **B** is similar to **A**, but fragmented and more repetitious. Instead of rhythmic displacement, I've created a call-and-response with the vocal for four bars. I'm going to keep the brass, but fragment them as well, so that they provide responses to the bass, who is responding to the vocal. The final *a* section, **B5-8**, is a copy and paste of **B1-4**.

Interval Games

Notice that every interval the brass play is either a 3rd or a tritone, with one exception—**B3** is a perfect 4th. These intervals give the brass a certain personality.

3rds are very stable; tritones are very unstable. Ya gotta love those opposites. When the saxes finally return in **B7-8**, they are welcomed like a long-lost friend.

To Repeat or Not To Repeat, That is the Question

Most songs are 32 measures long and last about a minute. This song is half that length, which makes us want to hear another chorus from the singer before we move on to the instrumental part of the chart. She's got two more sets of lyrics, so we could just repeat the background and save ourselves some time, and that could work out fine, but I had a different idea.

Switching Grooves

One of my favorite records I listened to in my youth was Ray Charles' *Mary Ann*. It starts with a groove and then switches to 4/4 swing—unleashing an exhilarating feeling of forward motion. How about if we do something like that? Switching grooves is one of the hardest things to execute successfully in jazz. Swinging is hard enough, but keeping the time constant from one groove to another and making it feel surprising and yet inevitable—that's a tall order. But I like a challenge.

The Second Chorus

At **C** (see *Score* p. 4/p. 191) we repeat the melody with slight adjustments to accommodate the words, however, everything feels completely different. The basic chord changes remain the same, but I'm going to take more harmonic liberties with passing chords and substitutions. The 4/4 swing groove takes our story to a whole new country. We've gone from a tight, controlled feeling to a loose and almost dangerous freedom. All of a sudden, we can't help but, as Count Basie used to say, pat our foot. Ah, the miracle of 4/4 swing.

Scoring the Rhythm Section

Someone once asked Duke Ellington how much information he gave the bass player. His answer was succinct: "As little as possible."

The goal in playing jazz is for the players to improvise a coherent conversation; each knowing his/her function and respecting all the other players, so that everyone can contribute at the highest level.

Don't tell the players what they already know.

As jazz players, we are trained to play 4/4 swing. Rhythm section players know how to function in that world. All you have to do is turn the drummer loose and give the pianist and bassist the chord changes. That's what they are most comfortable doing, and that's what they do best. I want to give them every opportunity to do that in my music. There are times when I need specific things

CARELESS LOVE – OCTET ARRANGEMENT

and I'm not afraid to ask for them, but when I can let them be who they are, I know it's gonna be swinging. Hence the very basic parts at letter **C**.

Dividing the Horns into Three Groups

At **A** and **B**, the horns were divided by brass and saxes. At **C**, the brass players remove their plungers and join the saxes for 5-part harmony (**C1**, and **C4-6**). They are answered by the three lowest horns (trombone, tenor and bari) in 3-part harmony, who are in turn answered by the two highest instruments (trumpet and alto) in unison. Each of these groupings functions like a different section of a big band.

Lead Lines

Notice that all the lead lines in letter **C** are almost completely diatonic. The only accidentals are the C# and F# lower neighbors. Writing simple, easy-to-sing lead lines makes the music more understandable to the listener and players alike. Harmonic interest can be created through chromatics in the bass and inside parts. In **C1** and **4-6** the top two parts are diatonic, and the three bottom parts move chromatically. I didn't plan this, but it happens often. Let's look at these harmonies.

Remember the original basic chords for this 8-bar phrase?

|| B♭ | F7 | B♭ | B♭ | B♭ | F7 | F7 | F7 ||

Dressing Up the Harmony

I'm going to dress things up a bit by adding some passing chords to create subtle movement and throw in a few chord substitutes for surprise, but ultimately all the chords resolve to the original chords that anchor the melody. Some of these harmonies are pretty wild, but they are all functional, and all the parts move melodically.

It starts with a strong relationship.

I wrote the trumpet lead part to relate to both the vocal and the basic chord progression. After that, I created a line for the bari and bass that implied substitute and passing chords. The bass plays quarter notes to establish the swing while the bari uses bass pitches concerted with the trumpet rhythms. The three inside parts wrote themselves. Since I already knew the root and two of the pitches for each chord, it was just a matter of filling in 3rds and 7ths, and maybe adding a 9th.

The Devil's in the Details

In **C1** let's work backwards from the final eighth note. The F13 is the anticipation of the F7 chord of **C2** and is approached chromatically from above. The trumpet pitches ascend while the other four parts descend, thus creating contrary motion which adds a little accent and attention to this last note of the phrase. The G♭7-5 is also approached chromatically from above by a Gm9. I especially like this voicing because it is symmetrical; G to D to A 5ths on the bottom, B♭ to F, forming a 5th on the top connected by the half-step between A and B♭. The Gm9 is approached chromatically from above by an A♭13. I like the oblique motion between the static F's in the trumpet and the descending notes beneath.

First and Last Chords

An interesting relationship occurred between the first and last voicings of this figure—the F13 shares the identical voicing with the A♭13, only transposed down a minor 3rd. This gives the phrase added continuity.

Your Next Question?

What's the relationship between the B♭ downbeat and the A♭13? My answer is: We don't care. As we learned from J.S. Bach, after the tonic chord, we can go anywhere and start our route back to the tonic. However, in this case, it should be noted that A♭7 (♭VII7) is a common substitute for the tonic (B♭). We will encounter this later.

Call-and-Response

There are a number of conventions in jazz that we can trace back to its beginnings 100 years ago and even earlier. There are breaks, stop-times, turnarounds, and more. None of these is as ubiquitous as call-and-response, which permeates every genre, period, and style of jazz and American popular music.

In **Careless Love**, I often have two or three levels of call-and-response going on at once. This is the case at **C**. The five horns respond to the vocal, then the three low horns respond to the five horns, and then the trumpet/alto unison responds to the vocal, the three low horns and the five horns. This is another example where the explanation seems complicated, but the music makes total sense when we hear it.

Writing Concerted Voicings with the Vocal

I generally try to avoid giving horns the same rhythm as the vocal, lest the words get obscured. This is especially true with trumpets. If the saxes and/or trombones are voiced below the vocal, it can work for a few notes. In **C2** the bottom three horns join the vocal for two 8th notes. I used contrary motion to secure their independence from each other; the horns ascend, while the vocal descends. The first 8th note (vox C) could be considered the top note of the horn F#° Drop 3 voicing. F#° is the *viio* of G minor. The horns move up stepwise into a Gm7 (no 5th in the voicing), while the vocal descends into a unison B♭, also stepwise. Normally we avoid unisons in writing counterpoint, except when using contrary motion. Gm7 *(vi)* is a common substitute for the tonic.

CARELESS LOVE – OCTET ARRANGEMENT

Introducing the Trumpet/Alto Unison

In **C3-4** the trumpet and alto play a unison response to the vocal. This line uses the jocular dotted 8th/16th staccato rhythms and is reminiscent of Dizzy Gillespie's *Birks' Works* (Birks was Dizzy's middle name—John Birks Gillespie).

Melody and Accompaniment

Rather than let two bars go by with no horn voicings, I continued the open voicings for the bottom three horns. The Gm7 resolves chromatically to the G♭7 (shoulder chord), which descends by half-step in the bass to a second inversion tonic B♭6/F. Note that the G♭7 voicing in the low horns omits the 5th, which is stated by the unison trumpet and alto. The same sort of thing happens on the resolution to the B♭6. The root is omitted in the lower horns and given on the next downbeat to the trumpet/alto unison. A beautiful thing about shoulder chords (*bVI7*) is that they can resolve to the tonic or to the dominant. Here we have the best of both worlds—it resolves to the tonic, but with the dominant in the bass.

Keeping the Form

After the trumpet/alto unison finishes their line, they rejoin the other three horns to resume their 5-part grouping. They are not due until **C5**, if they are to define the four-square form of the tune. By bringing them in a beat and a half early, we cover the seam. The form is still there, but it is less obvious.

Borrowing the Subdominant from the Blues

The use of the E♭13+11 in **C4** gives us a taste of the blues, where it is common to interchange tonic, dominant and subdominant—especially using ♭7's in the chords. This E♭7 serves as a *IV* chord as well as the dominant of the A♭13-9 coming up in **C5**. A♭7 (*♭VII7*) is a substitute for the tonic. Resolving it chromatically to G7 or by a 5th to D♭7 begins a cycle to get us back to our tonic (B♭). In this case the G7 leads to Cm7, chromatically down to B7. We need to hold back the tonic until letter **D** (two more measures. I used a series of downward chromatic triads in the low horns that finally get us to an F chord just before letter **D**. In music, as in sex, anticipation is at least half the fun.

Upper Structure Triads

The E♭13+11 in **C4** and the next chord (A♭13-9) are both voiced with upper-structure triads. The E♭7 has an F major triad above the 3rd and 7th (G and D♭), and the A♭7 also has an F major triad, but above its 3rd and 7th (G♭ and C). Upper-structure triads have a nice ring to them. Notice how the E♭7 uses a rootless voicing in the horns.

Afterwards, the bari plays the root on the bottom of each chord for the rest of this 8-bar phrase. Roots on the bottom add weight and stability. Starting with the A♭7 in **C5**, the next four voicings are all Drop 2 with an added root on the bottom.

CJCA III: WRITING FOR SMALL GROUPS

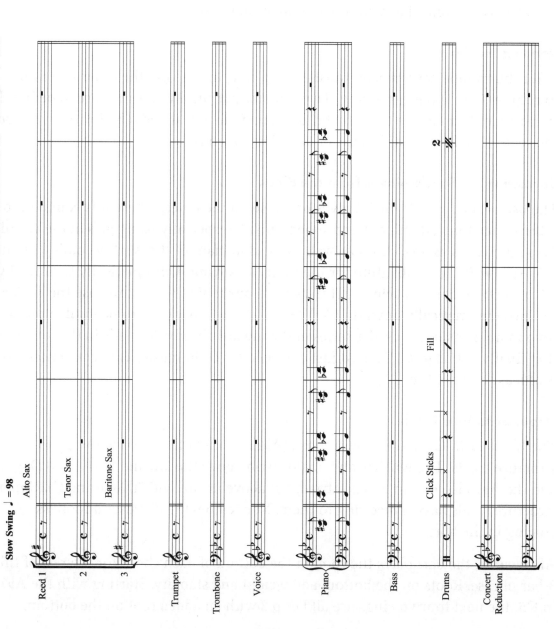

Example 11-1 *Careless Love* octet vocal score, page 1

CARELESS LOVE – OCTET ARRANGEMENT

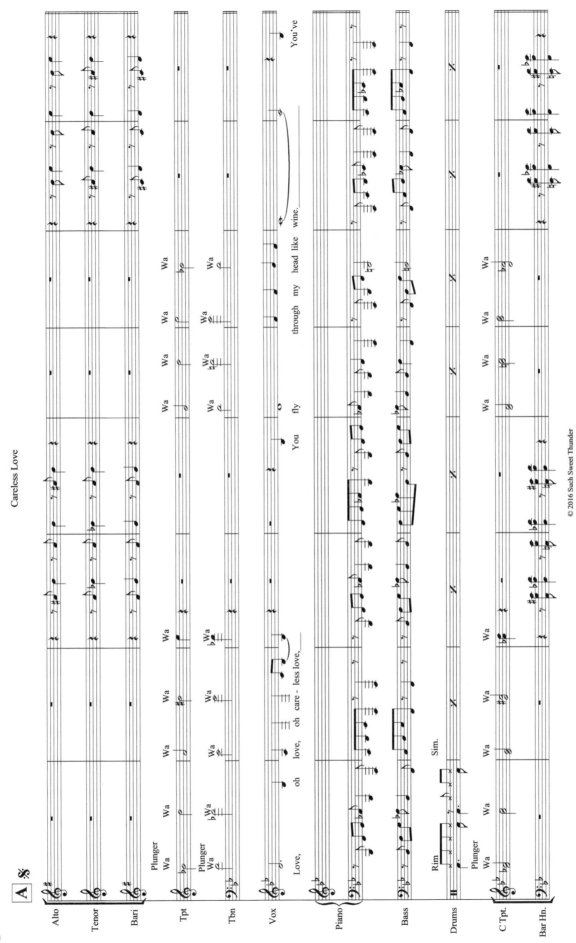

Example 11-1 Careless Love octet vocal score, page 2

CJCA III: WRITING FOR SMALL GROUPS

Example 11-1 *Careless Love* octet vocal score, page 3

CARELESS LOVE – OCTET ARRANGEMENT

Example 11-1 Careless Love octet vocal score, page 4

CJCA III: WRITING FOR SMALL GROUPS

Example 11-1 *Careless Love* octet vocal score, page 5

CARELESS LOVE – OCTET ARRANGEMENT

Example 11-1 Careless Love octet vocal score, page 6

CJCA III: WRITING FOR SMALL GROUPS

Careless Love

Example 11-1 Careless Love *octet vocal score, page 7*

CARELESS LOVE – OCTET ARRANGEMENT

Example 11-1 Careless Love octet vocal score, page 8

CJCA III: WRITING FOR SMALL GROUPS

Example 11-1 Careless Love octet vocal score, page 9

CARELESS LOVE – OCTET ARRANGEMENT

Example 11-1 Careless Love octet vocal score, page 10

CJCA III: WRITING FOR SMALL GROUPS

Example 11-1 Careless Love octet vocal score, page 11

CARELESS LOVE – OCTET ARRANGEMENT

Example 11-1 *Careless Love* octet vocal score, page 12

CJCA III: WRITING FOR SMALL GROUPS

Example 11-1 *Careless Love octet vocal score, page 13*

CARELESS LOVE – OCTET ARRANGEMENT

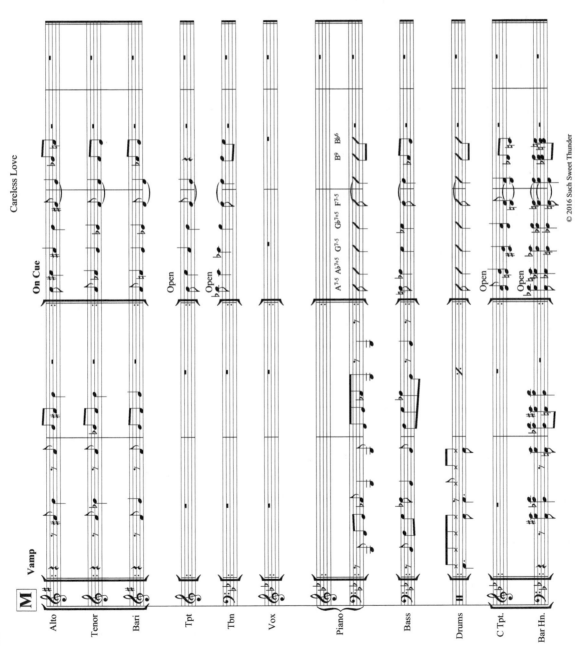

Example 11-1 Careless Love octet vocal score, page 14

Tensions appear in the top two voices, except for the Cm9 chord, which uses the same exact voicing as the Gm9 in **C1**, only transposed up a 5th. Reusing voicings gives the music continuity.

Answering the Vocal

In **C5-6**, the five horns answer the first two vocal downbeats with upbeats and then with two eighth notes—the same figure as the bottom three horns had in **C2**, only displaced earlier in the bar. We love when things come back, especially in unexpected places.

The Return of Dizzy's Line Accompanied by Descending Triads

Keeping the *aaba* form, I quoted *Birks' Works* again in **C7-8**. In order to accommodate the different chord change, I transposed it up to F7 and ended the line hinting at our old friend, the motif at **A** (7, 5, 7, 5, 1).

Sophisticated Triads

The remaining three bottom horns play a series of chromatically descending major triads voiced in open position. This is quite effective especially since the vocal holds out an F (the 6th of A♭, 7th of G, major 7th of G♭), and the trumpet/alto unison contains the 6th of A♭, the major and dominant 7th of G7 and the 6th and ♭5 of G♭. The beauty here is the purity and nobility of the major triads in open root position opposed to the melodic tensions. This disparity is at once contentious and harmonious.

Switching Gears for the *b* Section of the Tune

This bridge at **D** (see *Score* p. 5/p. 192) needs to be opposite from the material at **C**, but at the same time be developing our motifs. **D1-2** brings back the off-beats of **C5**, but instead of descending chromatically as before, we start by ascending (B♭ B7), descending (B7 B♭7) and then moving by tritone (B♭7 E7). The trumpet melodic line is made up of all tensions (major7, 13, 13, ♭5).

The Surprise of Sophistication

The B♭maj7 is a welcome respite from all the dominant 7th chords in this chart. The dominants provide a feeling of the blues in all their down-home funkiness. Major 7th chords on the other hand feel sophisticated and highbrow. After establishing the blues, major 7ths can be delightful.

Don't Git Sassy

When I was in high school, I came under the spell of Thad Jones's band and arrangements. It seemed to me that he created a feeling of the blues that permeated all his music. My favorite chart of his back then was *Don't Git Sassy*, a *Rhythm Changes* chart in D♭ with no bridge. After umpteen 8-bar choruses, the saxes would stand up and play their 16-bar soli with soprano lead. On the downbeat of the ninth bar something amazing happened that floored me. The soprano lands on a C for 2½ beats. How can that be? In all this blues-tinged music there is a long tonic major 7th chord in a prominent spot—and I like it. It feels appropriate and good.

Decades later Ralph Ellison turned me on to a book of his short stories. It's been 30 years, and although I remember loving all the stories, there is only one that I can recall now. The gist of it is that an executive of a major corporation is walking through the basement of his building and hears someone playing a symphony recording. He follows the sound and finally opens the door to the boiler room, and to his surprise, finds three or four Black janitors sitting and listening to Classical music on their coffee break. Did I mention that the executive is white?

Adding Repetition for Emphasis

D3-4 continues this pattern of tensions on top of chromatically ascending and descending open position voicings with roots and 5ths on the bottom. The E♭69 is a welcome relief from all the E♭7's (*IV7*) we've been hearing. Moving chromatically up to the E69 gives us the D♭ (enharmonic of C#) that we expected on the preceding E♭ chord. We then move back down to the E♭69. Each chord is repeated twice for emphasis. The *and*-of-4 and *and*-of-2 syncopations really grab our attention.

The Long and Short of It

After moving back down to the E♭69, the expected E° is approached chromatically continuing the 9th on top, which, in addition to the syncopation, creates a nice accent. However, the main thing we notice is that this chord is short—a short eighth note following all those long eighths. The switch is dramatic.

Tensions on Diminished Chords

I often like to use tensions on diminished chords, mostly but not exclusively in the top voice. Traditionally we derive these tensions from the diminished chord built a whole step above—F#° pitches for E° chords. If we have enough horns or fingers on the piano, we can play both chords at the same time F#°/E°.

Was Duke putting us on?

Herb Pomeroy, who taught a course called *Arranging in the Style of Duke Ellington* named this 8-note monstrosity *double diminished*. In 1968 one of Herb's prize students, bassist Paul Kondziella, joined the Duke Ellington Orchestra. At a certain point in the show every night, Duke would play a duet number with the bass. Paul would pick up his instrument and stand behind Duke while he accompanied the maestro. This one night, Duke lays into an D°/C° with four notes in each hand. Paul leans over Duke's shoulder and says to him, "Ah, double diminished!" To which Duke immediately turned his head to look directly at Paul and responded,

"Is that what that is?" Duke had been playing and writing such voicings for decades, but maybe had never had occasion to put a name to it.

Stuttering—Another Ellington Quote

The three unison E♭'s at the end of **D4** are a stutter effect. Added to the melody notes of the next measure, they form the opening motif of *Jeep's Blues*, composed by Johnny Hodges and arranged by Duke Ellington. Ellington featured Hodges on this tune for decades. The bottom three voices in open position bring back their 2-eighth-note response that we first heard in **C2** and **C6** (both in the second bar of those phrases). In **D5** they do it in the first bar of the phrase, thereby further obscuring the symmetrical phrase structure, but at the same time adding consistency.

And Now, For Something Completely Different

Similar to how we used major 7ths and 6ths where we had established dominant 7ths, **D6** is comprised of four long quarter notes. This is surprising on several counts:

With all the syncopation going on, outside of the walking bass line, we haven't heard many notes on the beat for this entire 16-bar chorus.

Any quarter notes up until now have been short. These are full value.

The striking dominants with upward chromatic melodic movement contrary to the other voices all descending chromatically.

Flat 9s on Dominants

Let's look closer at these voicings in **D6**. The bottom 4 voices form dominant 7ths with a +5. The trumpet resolves -9/+9, and then -9/+9 a whole step lower. What's really striking is the use of the ♭9. When I was a student of Herb's at Berklee, and then of Ray Wright at Eastman, the rule in class was "no -9s on tritone subs." In fact, on p. 11, I recommended that you not do it. Here I've done it twice in one measure, and it sounds great. Why?

I think there are two reasons: The ♭9's are diatonic notes, and they are coupled with the contrary motion with the other parts. Oblique motion could also make this particular dissonance work.

Tying The Package with a Bow Around It

The final two bars of this chorus **D7-8** is a cut and paste of saxes and rhythm section from the final two bars of the previous chorus **B7-8**. Lest you forget the previous chorus, this puts a nice perspective on the entire exposition of this chart.

[Let's listen to the chart from the top up to letter **E**. What we have is a simple earthy song with a bunch of fairly simple ideas assembled in a complicated way.

The question is: does it all hang together, or does the arrangement overpower the story of the lyrics?]

Solos

When I had my working octet in the early 2000s, I had some arrangements in which the solo section was left open, so that whoever needed solo space could be accommodated. Other charts would have specified soloists, but sometimes I didn't really have anyone in mind when writing the chart. Sometimes after playing charts with open solos, routines set in, or certain soloists sound so good on that tune, that we'd all be disappointed if they didn't solo.

Stop time vs. 4/4 Swing

With **Careless Love**, I didn't have anyone particular in mind, but I did want to preserve the binary presentation of the melody choruses. That is; one chorus with resistance, followed by a chorus of 4/4 swing (see *Score* pp. 6-9/pp. 191-194). The resistance on the blowing takes the form of stop time in the rhythm section. Each soloist plays a chorus over stop time before launching into a 4/4 swing chorus. The 4/4 swing could be extended by more choruses as needed. The main thing is that each new soloist starts with stop time.

Stop time

I could have just written one short hit per chord change for the entire stop time chorus **E** and **F**, but I was feeling that it would be fun to tease the listener a bit, hence the few measures of 4/4 swing (**E3-4**, **F4** and **F7-8**).

Blowing Changes

I kept the chord changes simple for the solo section. If the rhythm section wants to get fancy, it's up to them.

Shout Chorus

In a vocal chart, shout choruses are optional. Often the arranger will choose one of four options:

- Solo(s)
- Shout chorus
- Solo(s) and shout
- No solo or shout; the singer goes directly to her out-chorus (usually the last half of a 32-bar chorus)

It's also common for the final vocal chorus to modulate up a half-step or whole step to give the chart a lift.

In **Careless Love**, I opted to have a solo section followed by a shout chorus. Since the tune is short (only 16 bars), I can have the horns play 16 bars and then have the vocal take it out.

Sticking with the Ascending Half-step Motif and Rhythmic Displacement

This shout (see *Score* pp.10-11/pp. 195-196) is about strong, swinging rhythms. The upward half-steps are complimented by chromatically descending underparts until **I5**, where the ascending chromatic melody is accompanied in parallel motion (ascending minor 9th chords). Even the descending Cm9 arpeggio in **I7** utilizes a chromatic lower neighbor (B♮ resolving to C) before resolving to a B9-5 (a half-step above the tonic B♭, where it resolves on the next measure (**J1**).

Foreground Becomes Background

Letter **J** abounds with chromatic root movement. There continues to be upward chromatic movement in the melody in **J1** and **3**. **J3** has the identical melody as **J1**, but over totally different chords. When we hear this sort of thing, we experience the opposites of sameness and difference viscerally.

Diatonic Melody with Chromatic Harmony

The melody in the eight bars of letter **J** is completely diatonic, with the exception of four notes—all four happen to be blue notes (C#, C#, E, C#). For the first seven measures, this very sing-able line is harmonized with in 5-part harmony with the bari playing roots. **J8** is a transition back to the vocal chorus at **A**. To signal that transition, I pass the ball over to the saxes in 3-part harmony leaving the roots to just the bassist. The upward half-step in the alto creates contrary motion with the downward chromatics in the tenor, bari and bass; perfectly summing up what we've been hearing in **I** and **J**.

The Repeated Note Motif

J5 is the climax. It delivers the highest and loudest pitches in the chart. The repeated melody notes develop the repetition that has occurred earlier in the chart in **C1** and **D3-4**. We needed this idea to return to justify its being in the chart at all. The stutter on beat 4 of the next measure (**J6**) is further justification.

The Sweetness of a Delayed Resolution

J7 is the spot in the tune where both the melody and harmony normally resolve to the tonic. I've turned this full cadence into a semi-cadence to delay the resolution until the return of the vocal on the *D.S.* This creates suspense and makes the vocal feel all the more welcome.

Actually, **J7** is a development of **D6**. It's got the same melodic shape and starts with the same three melody notes, but the chromatic lower neighbor patern is broken in

J7 when with the A being a whole step above the previous G. The accompanying harmonies are all a half-step above those of **D6**.

I've also employed syncopation with short quarter notes as opposed to the on-the-beat long quarters of **D6**. But the most satisfying element about this measure is the least obvious—it upends the symmetrical structure of the song so subtly that hardly anyone would even notice; **D6** is an even numbered bar, while **J7** is an odd number. Both figures feel natural, and yet, clearly, **J7** is a bar late. Why do we like this so much? Consider this analogy:

The 1950s typical husband comes home late to face his angry wife, who has been trying to keep his dinner warm. Just as she starts to let him know how inconsiderate he is, he pulls a bouquet of flowers out from behind his back and tells her that he knew he'd be late for dinner, but he couldn't resist stopping off to buy her flowers to show how much he loves her. Naturally, all is forgiven—even better than forgiven. The anxiety of waiting was rewarded with an unexpected display of love and affection. Call me a romantic, but I just love stories with happy endings.

[Let's give a listen to our shout chorus **I** and **J**. Since we only have five horns, a screaming shout with the trumpet up high might be too much. If this was a big band chart, I'd certainly consider writing such a thing, but with no other trumpets to support him, the trumpet in this octet will feel awful lonely up there in the stratosphere. Maybe, let's just call this the Sock Chorus.

The questions I have for this part of the chart are:
   Do the players feel satisfied that they are integral to this chart?
   Does the audience feel satisfied that they got to hear all the horns together doing their thing?
   Have the motifs of the piece been developed sufficiently?
   Do we feel ready to hear the vocalist return, and even more important,
   are we hungry to hear her?]

That's It! The Chart's Done

Back in my classroom teaching days, I spent an entire day with one of my heroes, Gerald Wilson. The day started with Gerald teaching my arranging class. He brought in a few scores and recordings and explained how he approaches arranging for bands and singers. After listening to a chart he had written for Nancy Wilson, he took us through the score, telling us what he was thinking. There was the intro, she sings a chorus, then the band played half a chorus, at which point, he announced to us, "That's it! The chart's done." But Nancy still had a half chorus to sing; what about that?

Gerald explained that what was needed wasn't new material, but just to *D.S.* back and let the recapitulation simply repeat the exposition (or at least part of the exposition). Even his coda was pulled from earlier in the chart. He further explained that his goal wasn't to write as much as possible, but to be effective and relate to his audience; he needed to write as little as possible while holding everyone's interest.

The Recapitulation

Such is the case in **Careless Love** after letter **J**. We *D.S.* back to letter **A**, we repeat **A** through **D** before going to the Coda, where the material of **A** and **B** is repeated once more, but with new lyrics.

The Vamp

The vaudeville tradition of vamping until ready is a tried-and-true convention in just about all American music. In this case, directly following the last two bars of **K** (which is really just the last two bars of **B**), we repeat those bars until the cue to move on (see *Score* p.12/p. 199). If you can remember as far back as the intro to this chart, we used that same 2-bar phrase.

One More Decision

Very often vamps that come at the end of charts fade out. This is typically done as a board fade while mixing a recording. It's difficult to fade out in live performance. The decision to fade or create an ending after the vamp may have to be decided by how the chart will be performed: is it only for a recording, or will it be played live?

Providing a Button

In the case of vamp endings, I usually provide an alternate ending to follow the vamp. It's often just a button (single short note), but sometimes it can be a little bit more, which is what happened here. I certainly don't want to introduce anything new; that time has long since passed.

Cut and Past (I Mean Paste)

The most important parts of an arrangement are the first and last things the listener hears. Both should sum up the experience of the entire chart in as few measures as possible. Our intro succeeded in this respect. The same material also served us well for the vamp. Now what? For me, that was easy—I just thought of my favorite measure of the chart—**J7**. It summed up everything to that point. I cut and pasted that after the vamp. Since this figure ends on the dominant (F7-5), I'm going to need a tonic button to give me the finality a down home song like this demands.

One Last Chromatic

How about if, instead of a button, we add two 8th chromatic notes? Long, short! For the entire chart, the chromatic melody has often been in opposition to the underparts. All that contrary motion established a ton of conflict. We experience that once again in **L3** (see *Score* p. 13/p. 200). How about let's end with chromatic 6/9 chords in parallel motion? Finally, we agree! Well, almost. The trumpet just won't give up the ghost, but at least he's keeping his mouth shut.

[It's time to listen to the entire chart. How did we do? Does the music enhance the story the vocalist is telling? Is it sufficiently interesting to hold us for the entire piece? Is it distracting—leading us away from the words and the story? What's your emotion while listening? Do you feel sorry for the woman in the song—but also feel her strength? Does the music convey that? These are the really important issues that make or break this chart.]

12. Coda

Now that you know a lot of the details I think about when writing jazz for small groups, let's discuss the big picture. Here are my major thoughts about the medium:

- Keep the written parts to a minimum—less is more.
- The bulk of the development happens in the solos and their accompaniment.
- Honor the opposites.
- Don't tell the performers information they already know.
- Your job is to inspire the performers to be great.
- Learn the language, and then don't be afraid to express who you really are.

Creating art is not a contest. We aim high and fall short. That's to be expected. Always strive for excellence: pretty good is never good enough. Your best effort will reap its own reward. It's nice when others respect your work, but no award or prize will ever be as sweet as the process of creation. As they say, the true joy in life is the journey, not the arrival at your destination.

You know the expression, "The devil is in the details?" For an artist, the joy is solving all the minute problems inherent in those details. The innate logic you bring to these solutions relating each solution within a work of art to all the other solutions makes you an artist.

Anyone can solve problems, but an artist shows us a better world; a world where fairness prevails, and surprise delights us, where the opposites tantalize each other in every conceivable way, where we feel secure and loved, while at the same time we receive constructive criticism and learn to be better human beings, where art inspires us to be the people we secretly long to be—our highest selves.

You can live in this world but, as my friend Quincy Jones says, "You gotta leave your ego at the door." Meaning, stay focused on the music and its needs—don't be distracted by other considerations, like benefits the music might bring you.

I've been incredibly lucky having known and worked with many of the great composers, arrangers, musicians, singers, dancers, choreographers, actors, writers, and other artists of the past 50 years, but I've also had many disappointments along the way. The life of an artist is inherent with great highs and lows, but through it all, the hours I've spent sitting with a pencil in my hand or standing in front of a group of musicians have been my salvation. It is during those hours that all the troubles of the world do not exist for me. I am truly at one with the music. It courses through my veins as surely as blood and nerve impulses do.

CODA

When I was a young man, I studied yoga for a couple of years with a fine teacher. After attending a concert of mine, he told me that I didn't need to meditate—music is my meditation. It still is. Like other forms of meditation, it works best by letting go and with practice. If you have the courage to be honest, the world of music will be endlessly challenging and beautiful. You'll never run out of things to say or how to say them.

Not everyone will understand or even like your music. That's a given. What's important is that you like and believe in it, and keep striving for greater self-expression. You only have one product to sell in this life, and that is you. We want to know the real you. Don't hold back. Don't tell us stuff that someone else has already told us, or could tell us.

The reason that I wrote this book wasn't to teach you how to write like me, but to give you the tools and courage to write like you. It's time you got started. Don't worry about the first notes or measures. Just keep writing until the piece starts to form before your very eyes. It's not how the story begins but how it unfolds. We want to hear your story, as only you can tell it.

Ever onward and upward,

David Berger
May 19, 2023

Acknowledgements

First, I must thank my mother for the gift of music: for teaching me piano as soon as I was big enough to sit on the bench, and starting me on formal lessons when I was seven. Two years later I began playing trumpet in school. Why the trumpet? Louis Armstrong. At ten or eleven, I started studying piano with Stella Whitman, who taught me respect for the masters, and how to write Bach-style chorales. Under her guidance, I discovered that I was meant to write music.

Heartfelt thanks go to my lifelong buddy Bob Schwartz. Bob and I discovered and played jazz together from junior high school all the way through college. He has encouraged and supported me and my career in every way possible at every turn.

Many thanks to Bob's wife Nina, whose work as editor and graphic designer has transformed all my books from homemade to professional. Many thanks to Nikola Tomić for his meticulous editing, to Christian Dancy for his untiring help preparing the Sibelius® scores, and Leo Steinriede for posting the scores and videos online.

Throughout my career I've been lucky to have my music played by great musicians who breathe life and love into my little black dots. The personnel on the recordings for this book are:

Alto Sax, Clarinet, Flute:	Matt Hong
Tenor Sax, Piccolo, Clarinet:	Dan Block
Baritone Sax, Bass Clarinet:	Carl Maraghi
Trumpet:	Brian Pareschi
Trombone:	Wayne Goodman
Piano:	Isaac ben Ayala
Bass:	Sean Conley
Drums:	Jimmy Madison
Vocal:	Camille Thurman

The production team who lovingly transmuted our live sounds to digital:

Engineering:	Fernando Lodeiro
Mixing:	Oscar Zambrano
Mastering:	Peter Axelsson

Last, and certainly not least, I thank the many jazz composers and arrangers whose music has inspired me and taught me how to write, including Horace Silver, Benny Golson, Ray Charles, Duke Ellington, Billy Strayhorn, Quincy Jones, Duke Pearson, and Dizzy Gillespie. These masters created the language I learned to speak, and try to pass on to future generations.

Glossary

4-part close harmony (Also called *4-way close* or *block chords*): Voicings with four different pitches within the same octave, and containing a root, 3rd, 5th and 7th (or tensions of those pitches).

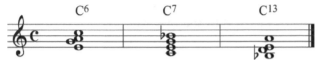

blue note: Notes from the blues scale that are approximately built on the ♭3, ♭5 and ♭7 of the home key. Jazz musicians will color these notes using bends and special intonation to evoke the feeling of the blues.

break: Within the context of an ongoing time feel, the rhythm section stops for one, two, four or even 8 bars. Most often a soloist will improvise during a break.

cadence: Where the music comes to rest at the end of a phrase. If a phrase ends with any chord going to V, it is a half cadence (semi-cadence). A half cadence is usually followed by a phrase ending in an authentic cadence.

call-and-response: Two parts engaging in a repeated question-and-answer format, usually of the same length. Usually played by different instruments or sections, as in Sousa's *The Stars And Stripes Forever*.

Charleston: The following rhythm:

chalumeau register: Lowest octave-and-a-half of clarinet, below the break.

chart: Arrangement or orchestration.

chromatic: Moving by successive half-steps. It can also mean non-diatonic.

coda: (Sometimes called the *outro*) A new section added to create a satisfying ending.

comp: To improvise accompaniment. Short for "accompany."

come sopra: As above.

concerto: Loosely, a piece that features a solo instrument. Traditionally concerti are three movements in length; the first movement being in sonata allegro form. Ellington's concerti *(Concerto For Cootie, Echoes Of Harlem, Boy Meets Horn)* are 1-movement sonata allegro forms, as is Strayhorn's *Charpoy*.

concerto grosso: A piece that features a small group of solo instruments within a larger ensemble. Ellington's *Jam-A-Ditty, Battle Of Swing* and *Launching Pad* are great examples.

constant structure: Transposing a voicing to follow the melody.

continuo: Improvised Baroque keyboard accompaniment that combines bass notes and chords.

contrary motion: Two or more voices moving in the opposite direction.

cross-sectional orchestration: Scoring for dissimilar instruments in unison or harmony, i.e. trumpet/tenor sax.

derby or hat: Metal mute for brass instruments in the shape of a derby. It may be fanned open and closed, or held still in front of the bell of the instrument, creating a distant sound.

diatonic chords: Those triads and 7th chords that occur naturally (with no accidentals) in major and minor keys. In jazz, although we use all seven chords and call them by number (I, ii, iii, etc), we normally only use the formal names for the tonic, dominant and subdominant (I, IV and V). Also in jazz, very often triads and 7th chords are interchangeable. The chord symbol "C" usually infers that we could add a 6th or a major 7th to the triad.

displaced rhythm: Starting a rhythm on a different beat or part of the beat.

dogfight: A back and forth quick call-and-response where both parts play the same repeated figure, usually separated by an octave and played by different instruments, as in Sousa's *The Stars And Stripes Forever*.

doit: An upward gliss (non-fingered portamento).

Drop 2: Semi-open voicings that are created by taking a 4-part close harmony and dropping the second voice from the top by one octave.

GLOSSARY

Drop 2 and 4: Semi-open voicings that are created by taking a 4-part close harmony and dropping the second and fourth voice from the top by one octave.

Drop 3: Semi-open voicings that are created by taking a 4-part close harmony and dropping the third voice from the top by one octave.

elision: Omitting the end of a phrase, so that the next phrase begins early.

fall-off: A downward non-fingered portamento. Fall-offs can be very short (also known as a Snooky Young fall-off—generally a half-step), short (a 2nd or 3rd) or long (an octave or so). Trombones use their slides, trumpets the half valve, and reeds a downward fingered gliss. The Snooky Young fall-off is lipped down by the trumpets and reeds. The trombones use fast slide movement. Fall-offs are non-measured and left to the discretion of the player(s).

fills: Melodic, chordal or rhythmic answers.

functional chord substitution: Replacing harmonies with other harmonies that conform to the tradition of tonic/dominant pull. The use of secondary chords (*ii, iii* and *vi*), secondary and applied dominants and chords borrowed from the minor modes (♭*III*, ♭*VI* and ♭*VII*), and some temporary modulations are also included.

groove: The composite rhythm. Generally refers to combined repetitive rhythmic patterns in the rhythm section, but may also include the horns. Standard grooves may be notated by name (bossa nova, swing, ballad, etc.). Manufactured grooves will either combine elements of two or more grooves (i.e. drums play swing, while the bass plays a tango) or wholly new elements, which will need to be notated specifically.

head: Melody chorus.

hexatonic voicings: Generally a triad stacked on top of another triad. Two very useful varieties are a minor triad over another minor triad built a major 7th apart and augmented triads built a major 7th apart.

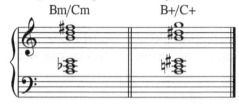

interlude: A contrasting form sandwiched between two chorus forms.

intro: Short for introduction.

inversion: Playing a motif upside down.

linearly derived harmonies: Harmonies that result from the confluence of melodic lines and don't conform to standard chord nomenclature.

mixed meter: Regularly changing the meter signature or implying a superimposed meter.

modulation: Changing key. There are four basic types of modulation:

sequential: Repeating the last figure starting on a different pitch and continuing in the new key.

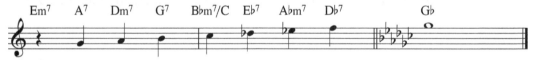

common tone: Holding over or repeating the last note from the old key to the new key.

dominant motion: Preceding the new key with its dominant or tritone sub of the dominant.

modulation, continued:

abrupt (sudden): No preparation.

motif: Short melodic and/or rhythmic fragment to be developed.

non-functional (color) harmonic substitution: Replacing harmonies with chords outside the key without preparation. This can include parallel harmonies, triads over non-related bass notes, etc.

oblique motion: One voice repeats a pitch or pitches while another voice or voices move in parallel and/or contrary motion.

octave displacement: Changing the octave of one or several notes in a phrase.

octave unison: Two or more instruments playing the same pitch or pitches but separated by an octave.

ostinato: A short melodic phrase repeated throughout a composition, sometimes slightly varied or transposed to a different pitch.

pad: Harmonized chordal background consisting mainly of notes of longer duration. It used to be called "organ background."

parallel motion: Two or more voices moving in the same direction.

passing chords (sandwich chords): Interjecting smooth harmonies to create interest and avoid static harmonies. There are four basic methods:

diminished: Determine the anchor chords, voice them with the basic chord, and then build diminished chords on the in-between notes (see example next page).

CJCA III: WRITING FOR SMALL GROUPS

chromatic (planing): If the melody moves by half-step or half-steps, determine the anchor chords, voice them with the basic chord, and then working backwards, move the underparts chromatically in the same direction as the melody.

dominant: Determine the anchor chords, voice them with the basic chord, and then working backwards, build dominant 7th chords a perfect 5th above the upcoming chord. Very often altered dominants and tritone substitutes are used.

diatonic: When the melody moves stepwise in the key of the chord change, determine the anchor chords, voice them with the basic chord, and then working backwards, move all the voices stepwise in the key in the same direction as the melody. This is the least used of the four approaches, so although it is simple and non-chromatic, it can sound fresh.

peashooters: Brass instruments with small bores. They create a brighter sound than the normal size horn.

pedal point: Sustaining or repeating a pitch while the other voices move. Using the dominant is the most common, but tonic pedal point is also used. Most often the pedal is voiced below the other parts, but it can also be on top (often called inverted pedal point) or in the middle.

GLOSSARY

pixie mute, plug: Originally called French straight mute or plug. A smaller version of the straight mute that fits in the bell of the horn beneath a plunger. A straight mute extends too far, and would prevent the plunger from covering the bell of the instrument.

plagal cadence: *IV I,* as in "Amen."

pyramid: Individual single note entrances that lay on top of the preceding entrances.

re-harmonization: Creating new harmonies to a previously existing melody. This can be a total re-vamping, isolated chords or something in between.

real sequence: Repeating a motif starting on a different pitch, and keeping all the intervals the same as the original. This results in stretching the tonality or leaving it altogether.

retrograde: Playing a motif backwards.

retrograde inversion: Playing a motif upside down and backwards.

ride pattern: The most common repetitive swing figure that drummers play on the ride cymbal. It can also be played on the crash cymbal or hi-hat.

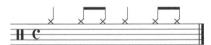

riff: Motif that gets repeated. Very often the harmonies change beneath it.

Schenkerian analysis: A method of musical analysis of tonal music based on the theories of Heinrich Schenker (1868–1935). The goal is to extract the underlying structure of a tonal work and to show how the surface of the piece relates to this structure. (from Wikipedia)

syncopation: Accenting the weak beat or weak part of the beat, while avoiding the following strong beat or strong part of the beat.

scronch: Accented quarter note on beat 4. It can be short or tied over into the next measure. Either way it gets the chord that belongs to the next beat.

sectional writing: Scoring for groups of like instruments, i.e. trumpets, saxes, etc.

serialization: The ordering of notes. Serial music limits the pitches to a specific set of intervals. Other elements can also be serialized, like rhythm, dynamics and orchestration. The goal is to create concise, integrated pieces. 12-tone music uses a row of all 12 chromatic pitches and serializes the intervals. Rows can and often do contain fewer notes (3, 4, 5, etc.).

shout chorus (also known as the *sock chorus*): The climax of the chart, where "everything comes together" and all the horns play.

slash chords: Generally triads over a related or non-related bass note. Sometimes triads or 7th chords over a different triad or 7th chord.

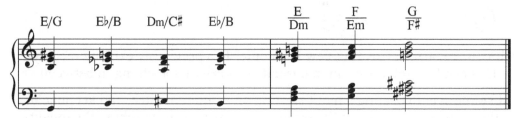

smear: Hitting a note flat and lipping up to the pitch. Alto saxophonist Johnny Hodges was legendary for this, but it is also used for expression on other horns and strings.

soli: A harmonized passage for two or more instruments playing the same rhythm.

song form: Generally 16, 32 or 12-bar forms (consisting of 4-bar or 8-bar phrases) that can be repeated and improvised on. The most common song forms in jazz nd the American Songbook are: *aaba, abac* (or *abab'*) or *aab* (the Blues).

song form notation: Lower case italicized letters represent phrases, i.e. *abcd*. Repeated letters mean that the material repeats verbatim or verbatim with a different turnaround, i.e. *aaba*. Letters with an apostrophe represent phrases that start the same, and then go somewhere else, i.e. *abab'*. Generally standard song phrases are 8 bars in length, but on rare occasions, they could be 4 bars, 6 bars, 10 bars, 16 bars, etc. Here are some examples of well-known songs with these forms:

abcd Stella By Starlight (8-bar phrases)

aaba Honeysuckle Rose (8-bar phrases)

aab The blues (4-bar phrases)

abab' There Will Never Be Another You (8-bar phrases)

abac Gone With The Wind (8-bar phrases)

aaba+tag Moonlight In Vermont (6-bar *a* sections, 8-bar bridge, 4-bar tag)

spread chords or chorale voicings: Open voicings that generally have the root on the bottom.

stop time: A regular pattern of short breaks, often filled in by a soloist. The melody chorus of *Sister Sadie* or the Harlem Globetrotters version of *Sweet Georgia Brown* are famous examples.

Glossary

stretto: The final section of a fugue, where the subjects occur in more rapid succession than previously, causing overlapping. The effect is to build tension, create a climax and ultimately lead to a feeling of finality.

subtone: Way of playing reed instruments very softly, usually in the lower register. The effect is that we hear more air than tone.

swing: The perfect confluence of rhythmic tension and relaxation in music, creating a feeling of euphoria. Characterized by accented weak beats (democratization of the beat) and eighth notes that are played on the first and third eighth notes of an eighth note triplet. Duke Ellington defined swing as when the music feels like it is getting faster, but it isn't.

tacet sheet: A part for an instrument that does not play a particular movement or piece. It has no notes, only the word TACET, and is used as a place saver.

symmetrical voicings: Generally 6- or 8-note voicings that, if divided in half, will contain all different pitches but the same intervals. The intervals can be in the same vertical order or inverted.

tag or tag ending: Derived from vaudeville endings. The two most common are ‖: IV#IV° I (second inversion) V#ii ii V :‖ I and ‖: iii V#ii ii V :‖ I. Repeats are optional.

tertian harmony: Harmony built in thirds.

tessitura: The general range of a melody or voice part specifically; the part of the register in which most of the tones of a melody or voice part lie.

thickened line: Voicings that are constructed from the melody down, with everyone playing the same rhythm as the melody. These kinds of voicings generally omit the roots and are not concerned with inversions, since the bassist is stating the root progressions.

thumb line: A slow moving (half notes or slower) mostly stepwise unison or solo line used to accompany a melody. Thumb lines stay away from melody and bass notes, and mostly contain 3rds and 7ths.

tonal (or diatonic) sequence: Repeating a motif starting on another step of the scale, but not adding accidentals, so that you are still in the original key.

tritone interval: A diminished 5th or augmented 4th. This interval contains three whole steps.

tritone substitution: Substituting a dominant 7th chord built a diminished 5th away from the original chord.

truncation: Shortening by lopping off the end of a motif, phrase, or passage.

turnaround: A series of chords that take us back smoothly to the first chord of a progression (usually the tonic). Although generally used to refer to the last two bars of an 8-bar phrase, *I vi ii V* and *iii vi ii V* are commonly called turnarounds wherever they occur.

tutti voicings: 4-part close ensemble voicings doubled throughout the brass and reeds. There are several variations, but the great majority fall into two categories: either the reeds double the trumpets in their register or an octave below. This is generally determined by the range of the lead trumpet. If he goes above the staff, the reeds are voiced an octave below.

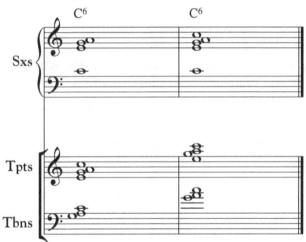

unison: Two or more instruments playing the same pitch or pitches in the same octave.

upper structure triad: A non-related major or minor triad placed above a 7th chord.

vamp: A repeated 2- or 4-bar chord progression usually supporting riffs. Coming from vaudeville, vamps are often used for intros, codas and interludes (especially just before a singer enters).

voicing: The specific pitches, inversion, and spacing that make up a chord.

Index

2-beat rhythm. 58, 61-62, 104
4-part close harmony. . .20, 94, 213-215
A-That's Freedom 144
absolute unison 85, 94
accents 34-35, 148-149,
    155, 185, 203, 219, 221
Adderley, Cannonball 127
Albam, Manny 119
American Songbook. . . 28, 30, 219, 230
appoggiatura 62
Arlen, Harold 1, 129
Armstrong, Louis 66, 212
arranging, definition 1
    goals 13, 30, 43, 126, 208
augmented triad 68, 216
authentic cadence 4, 5, 213
Axelsson, Peter. . . . . ii, 212
Ayala, Isaac ben. . . . . ii, 212
Bach, Johann Sebastian . . . . iv, 13,
    23, 186 212
Baron, Art. 97
bebop chord progression. . . 35, 83, 119
Berklee College of Music. 35, 204
Bigard, Barney. 43
Birks' Works 187, 202
Birth of the Cool 83
bitonality. 177-178
Blakey, Art. 99, 127
Block, Dan . . . . ii, 212
block harmony 20, 94, 213-215
blue notes. 16-17, 62, 78-79,
    130, 141, 206, 213
blues. 125, 130, 144, 148,
    179-181, 187, 202-204
Blues March. 144
bottom voices 95
break. 62, 85, 121, 123, 128,
    141, 149, 151-152, 186
Brookmeyer, Bob . . . . v, 30, 45, 63
Brown, Clifford. 65
Brown, Les 144
cadence 213
    a-men 4, 68, 85, 125, 175, 219
    authentic. 4, 5, 213
    bluesy 4
    plagal. 4, 68, 85, 125, 175, 219

call-and-response 44, 49, 58, 84,
    101-102, 124, 170, 182-183,
    186 213-214
change of texture. 69, 124, 153
change vs. repetition . . .59-60, 119, 124,
    129, 131, 149-150, 178,
    181, 184, 206-208
Charles, Ray 15, 179, 184
chorale voicings (spread chords) 23,
    142, 220
chord progression
    bebop 35, 83, 119
    blues . 19, 33, 62, 78-79, 125, 130, 148,
    179-180, 187, 202-204, 220
    diminished. 4, 8, 10, 16, 18, 25, 48,
    62, 80-81, 123, 180, 203
    Rhythm (I Got Rhythm) 105, 202
    modal 149, 151, 169
    Tin Pan Alley 105
    re-harmonization 13, 16, 18, 219
chords
    bebop style 35, 83, 119
    blues 4, 18-19, 33, 62, 78-79,
    125, 130, 148, 179-181,
    187, 202, 204, 213
    chromatic 16-17, 105, 142
    despair, *ivm* 16, 19, 175
    diatonic 3, 5, 6, 15-18, 26, 29-30,
    32-33, 49, 59, 62, 67-68, 78, 80, 104,
    121, 127-130, 141, 145, 154, 169, 172,
    175-176, 185, 204, 214, 218, 220
    diminished (diminished 7th) . . . 19, 25,
    217, 221-222
    dominant 7th 8-9, 11, 16-19
    22, 33, 103, 123-126, 172, 174,
    176, 202, 204, 218, 222
    dominant sus (dominant 7th #5)
    . . . . 21, 153
    double diminished 203
    inverted, inversions. . 18, 20, 24, 32-34,
    48, 68, 95, 218, 221-222
    major. 8, 19
    minor 4-8, 17, 19-23
    minor 7th 68, 105, 151
    minor 7th ♭5 (half diminished) 8,
    19, 62, 81, 131, 141
    minor, natural (Aeolian mode) . 7, 120

passing. 8, 15-16, 25, 42-43, 61,
    124-125, 175, 184-185, 217
root of 3, 9, 11, 13, 16, 18-21,
    23, 31-33, 35
secondary dominant. 8, 9, 11, 33
shoulder 146, 156, 187
subdominant. 4, 8, 11-12, 14,
    19, 105, 119, 148, 187, 214
substitute dominant 17
tonic substitute. 129
tritone substitution 10-11, 15,
    17, 48, 61, 94-95, 103, 126, 148-150,
    153-154, 175, 204, 216, 218, 222
climax of song
    highest note . . 29, 58, 60, 96, 146, 206
    shout chorus. 58, 60, 126, 145,
    173-175, 178, 205, 220
    widest interval 60
coda 63, 81, 97, 101, 126, 178,
    207-208, 213, 222
Cohan, George M. 27-29, 42
Cohn, Al 42, 45
come sopra 85, 211
complex vs. simple 79, 131, 142, 175
composing 1-2
concerto. 213
    concerto grosso 213
Conley, Sean . . . . ii, 212
constant structure 84, 105, 214
continuo. 214
contrary motion. 18, 31-32, 34,
    47-48, 58, 61, 67-68, 80-81, 84, 95, 97,
    102, 131, 144, 153, 176-177, 185-186,
    204, 206, 208, 214, 217
copy and paste . . .85, 120, 130, 178, 183
copying parts (extracting,
    engraving) 1, 219
counterpoint, contrapuntal 66, 121,
    149-151, 174-175, 177, 181, 186
cover up seams in the music . . 126, 152
Covert, Mary Ann. 94
Creative Jazz Composing & Arranging I
    (big band) . . . . v, 100, 228-229
Creative Jazz Composing & Arranging II:
    Writing for Singers . . . . v, 228-229
cup mute 149, 151, 174, 178
D.S. al Coda 97, 101, 126, 206-208

Dancy, Christian 2, 212, 228
Davis, Miles. 83
diatonic planing 176
diatonic sequence. 67-68, 221
diminished chord 8, 16, 19, 48,
        180, 203, 217
displaced rhythm 124, 181,
        183, 206, 214
dissonance 22-23, 47, 63, 79-81, 84,
      94-95, 122, 177, 204
dissonance vs. consonance. . . 47, 79, 94
dissonant Z-cell 24
dogfight. 214
doit. 214
dominant 7th chord 8-9, 11, 16-19,
    22, 33, 103, 123-126, 172, 174,
    176, 202, 204, 218, 222
dominant, secondary 8, 9, 11, 33
dominant, substitute. 17
dominant sus (dominant 7th #5)
 chord 21, 153
Don't Git Sassy. 202
Doodlin' 99
Dorham, Kenny 99
double diminished chord 203
dynamic markings. 34-35, 155, 170
Dynamic Sound Patterns of the Rod Levitt
 Orchestra, The. 98
dynamics. . . . 34, 143-144, 146, 155, 220
Eastman School of Music 204, 229
eighth notes, played legato 24
Ellington, Duke . iv-v, 1, 15, 20, 34, 43, 84,
  98-100, 126, 142, 155, 176-177, 179,
  182, 184, 203-204, 212-213, 221
Ellison, Ralph. 203
engraving (scribing) 1
engraving parts (copying, extracting) . . 1
Entry Of The Gladiators 144
escape tones. 85, 97
Evans, Gil . . . . iv-v, 83, 98, 172, 176
extracting parts (copying, engraving)
 1
fade out 208
fall-off 126, 215
Farmer, Art 127
fills 42
 drums notation. 42
Finale®. . . . . vi, 2, 35
form (song form) . . 1, 11, 28, 58, 62, 101,
  125-126, 128, 147, 180, 202, 216, 220
 aaba. 28
 aa'bc 11
 abac. 28, 101, 220

Forty-Second Street (song) 98
Foster, Frank. 58
Fuller, Curtis. 127
Gaslight 144
Gershwin, Ira 94
Get Happy 65
Gillespie, Dizzy (John Birks) . . . .v, 44-45,
        98, 187, 212
Golson, Benny . . . . . v, 65, 127, 144, 212
Goodman, Wayne. . . . . .ii, 97, 212
Gospel 15, 18, 127
groove, definition 215
groove, changing. . .58, 96, 143,-144 147,
    150-153, 157, 177-178, 184
Guy, Fred 34
Hamilton, Jimmy. 43
Harlem Nutcracker 97, 227
Harmon mute. 178
harmonic minor 5, 7-8
harmonization, harmony
 3-part 20, 141
 4-part jazz. 20, 48, 67, 80, 94,
    120, 122, 131, 141, 153,
    173-175, 214-215, 223
 5-part 82, 105, 124, 183, 185, 204
 basic 3-18
 diatonic. 3-5
 linearly derived 43, 216
 open, semi-open voicings . . 22-24, 94,
    101, 142, 187, 214-215, 220
head 42, 44, 48-49, 216
Heath, Jimmy 65
Hodges, Johnny. 204, 220
Honeysuckle Rose 148, 220
Hong, Matt . . . . ii, 212
Hubbard, Freddie 127
I Got Rhythm 105, 202
 Rhythm changes. 202
I Should Care 129
inner parts 11, 48, 154, 176
instrument range, tessitura 34, 45,
   49, 66, 82, 94, 174, 180, 221
 alto sax 82
 baritone sax 82, 94
 bass. 34
 flute. 174
 singer 180
 tenor sax. 49, 66
 trombone 66
 trumpet. 34, 49
instrumentation . . . 45, 65, 82, 151, 174

intro, introduction . 42, 44, 46, 48, 66, 69,
  83-85, 95, 100-105, 120-122, 126, 128,
  147, 150-151, 178, 181, 183, 207-208,
          216
intuitive, subconscious . .iv, 15, 29, 32, 60,
      66, 80, 171, 173
inversion, chord 18, 20, 24, 32-34, 48, 68,
      95, 218, 221-222
 mirror inversion 24
inversion, motif. 60-61, 68,
      78, 124, 129, 216
 retrograde. . 59, 61, 120, 141-142, 219
Israels, Chuck. 122, 228, 230
jazz march 144
Jazz Messengers, The . . . . .v, 99, 127
Jeep's Blues 204
Johnson, J.J. 65
Jones, Hank. 144
Jones, Quincy 174, 210, 227, 229
Jones, Thad . . . . v, 144, 202
Kellaway, Roger. 42-43
key signature 128-129
 choosing a key 180
Kondziella, Paul. 203
lead sheet, creating. 1, 11, 28
Levitt, Rod . . . . .v, 98
linearly derived harmonies. 43, 216
Lodeiro, Fernando . . . . ii, 212
Lone Ranger, The 100
Love for Three Oranges, The (opera)
 March 144
Lydian mode. 129
lyrics 28-29, 180-181, 184, 205, 208
 importance of 28-29, 203
Madison, Jimmy. . . . . ii, 212
Maraghi, Carl . . . . ii, 212
march, jazz 144
Marsalis, Wynton 1, 15, 43
Maxwell, Jimmy. iv
melodic minor 6
melody/accompaniment contrast . . 142
melody-bass relationship 31-32,
         61, 185
meter signature 34, 216
"Mickey Mouse" 43
Miley, Bubber 182
Miller, Glenn 144
minor 4-8, 17, 19-23
 harmonic. 5-8
 melodic. 6
 natural (Aeolian mode) 7, 120

INDEX

mixed meter 216
Mobley, Hank 99
Monk, Thelonious . . . . v, 43, 106
Morgan, Lee 127
motifs
    chromatic 44, 59-61, 63, 78-79,
                94-95, 102, 120, 123, 125
    combine 78
    develop under solo 123, 170
    development 44, 58-59, 69, 81,
           102-103, 119, 123, 125-126, 129, 131,
           141, 143, 145, 150, 169-171, 173-175,
           177-178, 202, 206-207, 210, 217
    pentatonic 44, 59, 61, 78-79
    retrograde . . 59, 61, 120, 141-142, 219
motion
    contrary 18, 31-32, 34, 47-48,
          58, 61, 67-68, 80-81, 84, 95, 97,
          102, 131, 144, 153, 176-177,
          185-186, 204, 206, 208, 214
    oblique 34, 47, 84, 95,
                131, 184, 204, 217
    parallel 18, 34, 153, 176,
                206, 209, 217
mute and instrument changes,
    notate 156
mutes
    cup 149, 151, 174, 178
    Harmon 156, 178
    plug, pixie 182, 219
My Ship 94
Nanton, "Tricky" Sam 182
natural minor (Aeolian mode) . . . 7, 120
notation
    don't over-notate 35
    drums, fill 42
    drums, groove 42
    give soloists time 156
    instrument or mute change 156
oblique motion 34, 47, 84, 95,
                131, 186, 204, 217
octave displacement 217
octave unison . . . 49, 58, 85, 95, 105, 120,
                123, 141, 217
Oliver, King 182
Oliver, Sy 84
On Green Dolphin Street 119
orchestrating, definition 1
ornamentation 78
pad 151, 155, 170, 217
parallel motion 18, 34, 153, 176,
                206, 209, 217
parallel voicings 84

Pareschi, Brian . . . . ii, 212
Parker, Charlie 45, 83
passing chords (sandwich chords) 8,
        15-16, 25, 42-43, 61, 124-125,
           175, 184-185, 217
    chromatic, planing 25
    diatonic 15
    diminished 25
    dominant 25
Pearson, Duke 144, 212
peashooters 218
pedal point 18, 34, 59, 218
pedals, dominant 31, 44
"pep section" 179, 181
plagal cadence . . 4, 68, 85, 125, 175, 219
planing 18, 84, 176, 218
    chromatic 18, 218
    diatonic 176
    parallel voicings 84
plug, pixie mute 182, 219
Pomeroy, Herb 203
Powell, Bud 99
Preacher, The 49, 99
Prokofiev, Sergei 144
quarter notes, played short 34
range of a composition . . . 82, 151, 221
range, instrument, tessitura 34, 45,
        49, 66, 82, 94, 174, 180, 221
real sequence 219
recap 63, 81, 101, 145, 178
reharmonization . . 15, 103, 129, 152, 154
repetition . 49, 60, 96, 103, 120, 126, 128,
      131, 145, 148, 156, 182, 203, 206
resolve, resolution 15-16, 43, 61, 79,
      95, 103, 125, 143, 172, 187, 206
Rhythm changes 105, 202
rhythmic displacement 124, 181,
                183, 206, 214
rhythmic unison 47-48, 58, 62-63
Richmond, Mike 42
ride pattern 218
Rising Storm, The 100
Room 608 49
root, chord 3, 9, 11, 13, 16, 18-21,
                23, 31-33, 35
    avoid in inside voicings 21, 35,
                83, 95, 187
Schenker, Heinrich 121, 172, 219
Schwartz, Marc 2, 228
scribing (engraving, extracting parts) . . 1
semi-cadence 11, 148, 155, 206, 213
Shiny Stockings 58

Shorter, Wayne 127
shoulder chord 146, 156, 187
shout chorus (sock chorus) 58-60,
      63, 79, 81, 97, 124, 126, 143-145, 147,
          173-175, 178, 205-207 220
Sibelius® . . . . vi, 2, 35, 181, 212, 231
Silver, Horace . v, 42, 49, 65, 99, 123, 127
Sims, Zoot 42-43, 45
sock chorus (shout chorus) 58-60,
      63, 79, 81, 97, 124, 126, 143-145, 147,
          173-175, 178, 205-207, 220
Solid Ground 98
solos . . . 42-44, 46, 58, 65, 151, 169-170,
                178, 205, 210
    background figures 44, 58
    backgrounds . 42, 58, 69, 78-79, 85, 95,
        122-123, 128, 142, 170-172, 217
    call-and-response 44, 58, 170, 213
    comping, accompaniment . . 42, 44, 69,
              122-123, 169-171
    give soloists time 156
    inspire the soloist 69, 79, 85, 123,
              169-171, 210
    send-off 44, 58, 101
    stop time 205, 220
Somewhere Over The Rainbow 129
song form 1, 28, 220
    aaba 28
    aa'bc 11, 220
    abac 28, 101, 220
song form notation 220
Sophisticated Hippie, The 99
Soul of the City 119
Sousa, John Philip 65, 144, 213-214
St. Louis Blues March 144
stop time . . 104, 128, 141, 186, 206, 230
Stravinsky, Igor . . . . iv, 1, 98
Strayhorn, Billy . . 126, 142, 148, 155, 169,
            176-177, 212-213
Streamlined Sibelius® . . vi, 2, 181, 228, 231
stretto 60, 221
subconscious, intuitive . . iv, 15, 29, 32, 60,
                66, 80, 171, 173
subdominant chord . . 4, 8, 11-12, 14, 19,
              105, 119, 148, 187, 214
subito p 34, 155
subtone 66, 221
swing . . . . v, 34, 125, 144-145,
      147, 149, 169, 173-174, 181,
      184-185, 205, 215, 219, 221
symmetrical voicings 24, 221

syncopation 20, 30, 58, 62, 79, 102, 104-105, 123, 144, 150, 181, 203-204, 207, 219
Take The "A" Train 44, 148
tension and release 22, 33, 43, 46-48, 61, 63, 79-80, 174, 177
texture change 69, 124, 153
thickenii, 210 melody line . . . 20, 23, 221
thumb line . 141-142, 151, 154-155, 170, 173, 221
Thurman, Camille . . . . ii, 212
tonal sequence (diatonic sequence) 67-68, 221
tonic chord 3, 5-6, 8-9, 11-20, 25
transcribing 1-2, 65, 152, 229
  how to 2
transposing the score 35
triad, augmented 68, 216
triads 3, 15, 19-20, 32, 33, 67-68, 80, 85, 94, 104, 122-123, 182, 187, 202 214, 216-217, 220, 222
tritone interval 62, 150, 221
tritone substitution . . . 10-11, 15, 17, 48, 61, 94-95, 103, 126, 148-150, 153-154, 175, 204, 216, 218, 222
  avoid flat 9ths on 95

trombone, writing for 65-69, 79-80, 141, 146, 149, 174, 182-183, 185-186, 215
  slide problems 65
trumpet-bass relationship 33
turnaround 84, 95, 149-150, 186, 220, 222
Ulehla, Ludmila 43
unisons 31, 46, 49, 61, 63, 83, 85, 104-105, 131, 141, 151, 186
  absolute 85, 94
  avoid in counterpoint 186
  octave . . . 49, 58, 85, 95, 105, 120, 123, 141, 217
  rhythmic 47-48, 58, 62-63
upper structure triads 187, 222
vamp 178, 208, 219, 222
  alternate ending after 208
vibrato 155
voice leading 22-23, 47, 96, 175
  parsimonious 47
voicings, definition 20
  3-part harmony 20, 141
  block harmony (4-part close) 20, 94, 213-215
  chorale voicings 23, 142, 220
  cluster voicings 24

constant structures 84, 105, 214
dissonant Z-cell 24
Drop 2 . . . 22, 102, 120, 123-124, 173, 175, 187, 214
Drop 2 & 4 . . . . 23, 215
Drop 3 . . . . 22, 173, 186, 215
like intervals, voicings of 24
mirror inversions 24
open voicings 22-24, 94, 101, 142, 187, 214-215, 220
parallel (planing) 84
semi-open 22-23, 214-215
symmetrical 24, 221
thirds and sevenths 47, 49, 82
unstable 19, 68, 154, 184
Waller, Thomas "Fats" 148
Weill, Kurt 94
Whetsol, Arthur 182
Wilson, Gerald 207
Wilson, Nancy 207
Woodman, Britt 97
woodwind doubles 151, 174
Wright, Ray 23, 95, 204
Yankee Doodle Dandy (musical) 27
Zambrano, Oscar . . . . ii, 212

About the Author

Jazz composer, arranger, and conductor David Berger is recognized internationally as a leading authority on the music of

Duke Ellington and the Swing Era. Conductor and arranger for the Jazz at Lincoln Center Orchestra from its inception in 1988 through 1994, Berger has transcribed more than 1000 full scores of classic recordings, including more than 500 works by Duke Ellington and Billy Strayhorn. Several of these transcriptions, and a number of original arrangements, were featured in the in the Broadway hits, *Sophisticated Ladies* and *After Midnight.*

After five years writing and playing trumpet with the Alvin Ailey Dance Theater, in 1996 Berger collaborated with choreographer Donald Byrd to create and tour **Harlem Nutcracker**, a full-length two-hour dance piece that expands the Tchaikovsky/Ellington/Strayhorn score into an American classic. The 15-piece band assembled to play this show has stayed together as the David Berger Jazz Orchestra. The DBJO has recorded six CDs and actively performs Berger's music on tours throughout the United States and Europe

Berger has written music for every conceivable configuration of instruments from solo piano to symphony orchestras. His music has been featured on television, in numerous Broadway shows and films. His arrangements and transcriptions are played by thousands of big bands around the world.

He has composed and arranged for the Duke Ellington Orchestra, Jazz at Lincoln Center, Quincy Jones and the WDR Big Band among others. Berger's special fondness for for singers has led him to compose and arrange for such leading vocalists as Jon Hendricks, Betty Carter, Natalie Cole, Rosemary Clooney, Madeleine Peyroux, Cécile McLorin Salvant, Kathleen Battle, Jessye Norman, and Susan Graham.

For 30 years Berger taught jazz composition and arranging in addition to coaching ensembles at Juilliard, Manhattan School of Music, William Paterson University, and the New School. He continues to conduct numerous high school, college, and professional big bands and radio orchestras throughout the US and Europe.

In 2008 he recorded an octet album of his adventurous arrangements of Harry Warren songs featuring saxophonists Harry Allen and Joe Temperley. This book explains in detail how to create jazz arrangements and compositions that are personal expressions, inspire the performers to be great, and thrill audiences.

www.SuchSweetThunderMusic.com

Other Books by David Berger

- *Creative Jazz Composing & Arranging*
- *Creative Jazz Composing & Arranging II: Writing for Singers*
- *Life in D♭: A Jazz Journal*
- *High School Jazz: A Director's Guide to a Better Band*
- *Fancy Footwork: The Art of the Saxophone Soli*
- With Chuck Israels:
  The Public Domain Song Book
- With Christian Dancy and Marc Schwartz:
  Streamlined Sibelius®

CDs are available from **SuchSweetThunder.com** and **Amazon.com**. Downloads can be purchased at those outlets as well as **CDBaby.com**. Downloads and streaming are available at all online digital outlets.

CDs by David Berger

- *Harlem Nutcracker* / David Berger & The Sultans of Swing
- *Doin' the Do* / David Berger & The Sultans of Swing
- *Marlowe* / David Berger & The Sultans of Swing
- *Hindustan* / David Berger & The Sultans of Swing
- *Champian* / Champian Fulton with David Berger & The Sultans Of Swing
- *I Had the Craziest Dream: The Music of Harry Warren* / David Berger Octet
- *Sing Me A Love Song: Harry Warren's Undiscovered Standards* / David Berger Jazz Orchestra with Freda Payne and Denzal Sinclaire
- *Old Is New* / David Berger Jazz Orchestra with Denzal Sinclaire (Download Only)

Available for download from **cdbaby.com, iTunes.com, allmusic.com, Amazon.com,** and **SuchSweetThunderMusic.com**.
You can find many jazz arrangements, compositions and transcriptions at **SuchSweetThunderMusic.com**.

Book Reviews

Creative Jazz Composing & Arranging, Vol. I

David Berger shares the secrets of writing music that's fresh, original and memorable, distilled from a lifetime of composing and arranging for the iconic bands of Quincy Jones, Wynton Marsalis and the Jazz at Lincoln Center Orchestra. Downloadable complete scores and recordings are included.

"I love this book. The discussion of the musical content is clear and concise, while a respect and passion for the music and the creative process are evident throughout. The big band scores are brilliant—steeped in the rich tradition of jazz, but also conveying the unique musical character that is David Berger.

It is a joy to get inside the head of one of my favorite jazz writers and bandleaders."

Bill Dobbins
Professor of Jazz Composition and Arranging
Eastman School of Music

Life in D♭: A Jazz Journal

David Berger, renowned jazz composer, arranger, band leader and educator, tells you what it's like... from falling in love with jazz as a boy, to his first jobs as a musician and arranger... from international triumphs with the Jazz at Lincoln Center Orchestra, to heartbreak and success with his own Big Band. The chapter on transcribing alone is worth the price.

"David tells it like it is. A compelling read for every musician and music lover."

Quincy Jones
Producer/musician/composer/arranger

High School Jazz: A Director's Guide to a Better Band

The culmination of 40 years of teaching jazz, with proven techniques to help you bring a band to its highest potential.

"I have been a high school jazz band director for 21 years, and this is the best book I've ever seen about teaching jazz band. If you want your band to sound authentic and swing hard, study this book from cover to cover. Guaranteed to make your band better!"

Josh T. Murray
Jazz Band Director
Rio Americano High School, Sacramento

CJCA III: WRITING FOR SMALL GROUPS

Creative Jazz Composing & Arranging, Vol. II:
Writing for Singers

"David Berger's new book *Writing for Singers* is a goldmine of valuable information on how to write and arrange music in a way that perfectly balances song, singer, and band. The insights in the opening pages, by Berger and lyricist Paul Mendenhall, convey a deep love and understanding of the Great American Songbook.

Berger has combined songs from the 1910s-1930s, with several of his originals (with lyrics by Mendenhall) in a variety of tempos, moods, harmonic schemes, and orchestrations for big band and vocalist. The music is superbly delivered by vocalist Denzal Sinclaire and David's big band.

Each chapter leads the reader clearly through the process of creating an arrangement from lead sheet to finished score. Each transposed score page includes a condensed C-score reduction at the bottom.

As in the first volume of this series, Berger's anecdotes of the professional jazz scene are insightful and entertaining. His description of the creative process, like his arrangements, reflects the gamut of the human experience with warmth and charm."

Bill Dobbins
Professor of Jazz Composition and Arranging
Eastman School of Music

"Dave Berger's **Writing For Singers** is as thorough a study of the craft and art of writing band arrangements for singers as I've seen, and it contains a wealth of information on the art of songwriting as well. There are beautifully performed and recorded examples (including exceptional performances by the fine singer, Denzal Sinclaire), full scores, concert score reductions and extraordinarily detailed analyses of everything that went into the creation of these works.

Composers and arrangers develop habits of thinking and working that lurk partly below our consciousness, allowing us to write intuitively without slowing or stopping to intellectualize every decision. David is a particularly fast and intuitive writer/arranger. His songs and arrangements have taken him far less time to create than the analyses he presents here. He has meticulously dissected his ideas, described them in detail, traced their inspirations and assessed their effectiveness.

Little of this analytical activity surfaces when he's doing the musical work. It takes patience and profound attention to examine your own work and extract from it the things you might not have even realized you were thinking in its creation; all the things you think might be useful to someone learning the craft you have internalized. David has done this with thoroughness, clarity, and humor. It's hard for me to imagine anything important he's left out. This book is an invaluable resource."

Chuck Israels
Composer/Arranger/Bassist

The Public Domain Song Book

I'm regularly looking for public domain tunes to arrange for beginning to intermediate instrumentalists. The best tunes are those for which numerous recordings exist that students can play along with, particularly early jazz standards. Berger and Israels have simplified a process that normally involves either relistening to copious amounts of old music, or scouring online archives like IMSLP (International Music Score Library Project) or the Library of Congress.

The value of this book, however, is the accessibility, and clear, thoughtful copy-editing. It just makes my job that much easier. Finally, in an age where songwriters are dragged into court for copying someone else's chord changes(!), a book dedicated to public domain music is a godsend.

Nathan Botts
Trumpet Player, Educator
Winner, Jazz and Classical Solo Competitions, International Trumpet Guild
Band Director, Phoenix Country Day School

Streamlined Sibelius®

I'm an experienced Finale® and Dorico® user with only limited Sibelius® experience, so I decided to take the plunge and use David's book to get my Sibelius® skills up. All the walkthroughs are very clear, with an easy-to-follow organizational structure, especially for a Sibelius® novice like myself.

This is quite a unique book because it's a both a Sibelius® how-to manual and a music notation style guide all in one! There are many books that deal with one or the other, but David combines the two in a way that reflects his decades of experience in the music business. Many of the best notation guides that address jazz notation, like Clinton Roemer's *The Art of Music Copying*, are long out of print, so this book is an excellent way to learn both what the accepted practices are for professionally engraved music, and how to do them in Sibelius.®

This book is a fantastic new resource that I'm sure I'll refer to over and over, and I'd highly recommend it to anyone looking to improve their Sibelius® skills.

Todd Bashore
Arranger, Composer, Saxophonist

Made in United States
Troutdale, OR
03/14/2024

18451260R00133